Dear Marilyn,

by Marilyn Hickey

Dear Marilyn,

by Marilyn Hickey

Marilyn Hickey Ministries
P.O. Box 17340
Denver, CO 80217

Unless otherwise indicated,
all Scripture quotations are taken from
the *King James Version* of the Bible.

ISBN 1-56441-006-4

Printed in the United States of America
Copyright © 1985 by Marilyn Hickey
All Rights Reserved

CONTENTS

Chapter One
Spouses and Marriage 7
- Should Wives Submit to Unsaved Mates? 9
- Who Controls the Money? 10
- Is There Marriage After Children Leave Home? 11
- The Right Christian Man? 12
- Can a Wife be a Minister? 13

Chapter Two
Children 17
- Spanking—Yes or No? 19
- Abusing Privileges at Home 21
- Child With Poor Self-Esteem 22
- Unsaved Children 24
- Child Who Rebels Against Church 26

Chapter Three
Friends and Relatives 29
- Unsaved Relatives 31
- Ridicule by Unsaved Family 33
- Friends in False Doctrine 34
- Possessive In-laws 36
- Death of Unsaved Loved Ones 37

Chapter Four
Sex 41
- Virginity—Old Fashioned? 43
- Living In Sin 44
- Adultery—Just Once? 45
- Unclean Thoughts 47
- Improper Teacher-Student Relationship 48

Chapter Five
Personal Problems 51
- Unholy Temper 53
- Quitting Smoking 54
- Bad Influences from Others 56
- Weight Control 57
- Self-Condemnation 59
- Overcoming Putdowns 60

Chapter Six
The Bible 63
- Which Bible Translation Should I Read? 65
- Bible Reading Consistency? 66
- When is the Tribulation? 68
- Spirit, Soul, and Body—Which is Which? 69
- Is Loud Prayer Scriptural? 71

Chapter Seven
Prayer 73
- Prayer Length 75
- Determining God's Voice 76
- Healing Prayers 78
- Long Distance Prayers 79
- Loud or Silent Prayer? 80

Chapter Eight
Sin 83
- Sin Unto Death 85
- Regret vs. Repentance? 86
- Suicide 88
- Abortion 89
- Confrontation of Sinners 92

Chapter Nine
The Movement of God 95
- How Can I Know God's Will? 97
- How Can I Cast Out Demons? 98
- Why Does Healing Take Time? 100
- How Do I Bless my Enemies? 101
- Do Words Work? 102

Chapter Ten
The Body of the Church 105
- Has the Charismatic Movement Crested? 107
- Can Women Be Deacons? 107
- Should the Church Help the Poor? 109
- Minister: How Can I Fight Criticism? 110
- What About Water Baptism? 112
- Can Divorcees Be Part of the Church? 113

Chapter Eleven
Pastors and Ministries 115
- Discontentment With Pastor and Congregation ...117
- Pastor Outside the Scriptures 118
- Evil Gossip About Ministries 119
- Wearing Other Ministers' Mantles 120
- Choice of Leaders in Ministry 122
- Lazy Assistant Pastor 123

Chapter Twelve
Unchristian Christians 125
- Carnal Christians 127
- Up-and-Down Christians 128
- The Backslider and Salvation 130
- Materialistic Christians 131
- Unchristian Christians 132
- Prophecy or Misdirection? 134

Chapter Thirteen
Miscellaneous Things 137
- Food for the Communists 139
- Wasted Time 139
- Dealing with Correspondence 142
- Loser or Winner 143
- Make-up for Christians 145

Index 149

Dear Marilyn,

Chapter One
SPOUSES AND MARRIAGE

- Should Wives Submit to Unsaved Mates?
- Who Controls the Money?
- Is There Marriage After the Children Leave Home?
- The Right Christian Man?
- Can a Wife be a Minister?

SHOULD WIVES SUBMIT TO UNSAVED MATES?

Dear Marilyn:
My husband is trying to make me stop serving God. I really don't know how to handle this pressure. The Bible says that wives are supposed to submit to their husbands. My husband has told me several times that I must stop reading my Bible and going to church. I have prayed a great deal about this situation, but it's getting worse. I want my husband to be saved, but how can I win him by fighting with him?

Dear Friend:
God has told us that we must seek first the Kingdom of God and His righteousness. When we seek Him first, all the rest of our hearts' desires are added to us. I am telling you that your submission to God should precede your submission to your husband. But don't throw out the baby with the bathwater—there is a way to handle your situation.

When my mother became a Christian, she received the baptism of the Holy Spirit, and it was quite a shock to our household. My father was angry at first. He exploded, "I don't want you to have anything to do with the Bible or that church!" But my mother didn't give up. She explained to my father, "From now on I will be a better wife. I'll be more in love with you than I have ever been. Our life together will be better than it has been. But on Sunday mornings I am going to church, and I am going to read my Bible every day so that I can be a better wife."

My mother never backed down on her commitment to God, and as a result, her family was saved. Today my father is in heaven, and my brother and I are serving God.

Why?--because my mother submitted FIRST to God and second to her husband. Because of her stance, miracles came to our household. Submit to God's call first and then to your husband as a wife. You'll have miracles, too!

WHO CONTROLS THE MONEY?

Dear Marilyn:

I don't know how much longer I can take my husband's restrictions on the money I spend. He insists that I buy only secondhand clothes or accept clothes that are given to us. Yet he thinks nothing of spending money for camping equipment, guns, or boats. By the way, I have a full-time job and feel I deserve some say in how our money is spent. I am a Christian and I don't like to fight—especially when I think I'm going to lose! But how else can I resolve this matter?

Dear Friend:

As always, honesty is the best policy between you and your husband. I want to ask if you've really spent time praying about this situation. Have you put your hurt emotions in line with God's Word? That is your number-one preparation before you approach your husband to discuss this sensitive subject.

My husband and I faced a similar situation in our early years of ministry. It seemed that no matter what I bought to wear, my husband said, "That is too expensive." He wanted me to look attractive, but he didn't want me to spend any money.

At the time, I was working full-time, just as you do. And—like you—I felt bitter and resentful toward my husband. Every time he started griping about how much I had spent, I would retaliate by screaming back, and we would end up in a big fight. That certainly was not the answer!

Finally the Lord spoke to me, "Your problem is that you think your husband is your source. I am really your Source. If you will discuss this problem with your husband in an attitude of love and faith, I can change his heart."

I prayed intensely, preparing myself to discuss the situation with my husband. Then I went to him and said, "Pray for me." His eyes widened and he asked, "Why? What is wrong?" I answered, "I have a bitter spirit toward you." With those words, my husband almost fell over backward! Then I brought up his attitude about the way I spent money. I said, "If I am wrong, I want to pray about this bitterness so that I will be willing to follow your direction. But if you are wrong, you need to repent."

My husband and I prayed, and God really blessed our moments of honesty together. From that time on, my husband stopped complaining about my clothing. After all, clothing is a necessary expense. But remember, the change did not come because I dealt with him. It came because God dealt with him.

Your mate isn't your source. God is your Source, and He will direct your mate's heart to line up with the Word. Pray and then approach your spouse in a spirit of love and honesty. As you listen to the guidance of the Holy Spirit, I know that your problem will be resolved.

IS THERE MARRIAGE AFTER THE CHILDREN LEAVE HOME?

Dear Marilyn:
My husband and I have been married for 24 years. Our

youngest child will enter college this fall, and then we will have no children at home. It bothers me when I think of my marriage relationship devoid of children. Am I just walking in fear? What will our life be like together without children? For so many years our lives were centered on our children. I just can't imagine making this adjustment. Maybe this sounds foolish to you, but it is very serious to me.

Dear Friend:
Recently my husband and I celebrated our 30th wedding anniversary. We had our daughter later in life, so we are still looking forward to another year and a half of her being with us before she enters college. But Sarah had a week away from us at a basketball camp, so we had a little taste of what it would be like not having any children at home. Frankly, we had a delightful time with each other. It was like courting all over again! I thought, "We had a wonderful marriage before we had children. Children have simply enhanced our relationship. And when they are gone, our relationship will continue to flourish."

When Jesus turned the water into wine at the marriage in Cana, the governor exclaimed, "You have saved the best wine for last!" I believe that the best wine of marriage is the last! Wine grows better with age, and I believe that marriage can grow better with age. The miracle performed at the wedding in Cana certainly was an important occasion. It was the beginning of Jesus' ministry upon the earth. I believe this miracle pictured Jesus' spiritual union with the Body of Christ, plus it showed that our love and fellowship with Him can grow better and better.

Certainly our marriages are patterned after Jesus' marriage to His bride. I believe you can look to Jesus and be confident that your marriage will keep getting better. I believe that the best is yet to come! Remember, Jesus saved the best wine for the wedding feast and for your marriage, too!

THE RIGHT CHRISTIAN MAN?

Dear Marilyn:

How can I meet the right man? I am a college graduate in my early thirties. I was not really ready to marry until two years ago when I received Jesus as my Savior and was baptized in the Holy Spirit. I am much more settled now than I was before, and I believe that I could now make someone a good wife.

But where do you find Mr. Right? I feel left in the lurch because there are very few young, single men in our church. Do you believe in computer dating services to find a mate? Do you think that Christians should use those services?

Dear Friend:

Number one—and I mean **number one**—do you want God's perfect plan for your life, or do you want something else? There is no question that God has a Mr. Right for you. But a computer is not the source for your answer. A computer will not find a husband for you, but the Holy Spirit will! The Holy Spirit leads you to truth. Scripture tells us that we are not to be unequally yoked with unbelievers. A computer could care less whether you are matched with a Christian or not. Computers simply try to find mates that have compatibility in the soulish area. As a believer, you will want someone who can be one with you—spirit, soul, and body!

You are now the temple of God (1 Corinthians 3:16). In Matthew 12:25b Jesus said, *"Every kingdom divided against itself shall not stand."* So it is important that you find a young man who is saved and spirit-filled. Then you will have a house that is united and will stand!

I am going to give you a simple Bible formula for finding the right mate:

Number 1. Put God and His plan for your life first—don't put your desire for marriage first. Jesus said to *"seek ye first the kingdom of God, and his righteousness, and all of these things shall be added unto you"* (Matthew 6:33). If you put Jesus first, as I believe you have, then God will add what needs to be in your life. God is the One who has given you a desire to marry, and I believe He can fulfill that desire if you are patient.

Number 2. Don't let the enemy scare you with the idea that you will lose if you don't accept the first available male. Remember, the devil drives the sheep; Jesus leads His! And you are Jesus' precious lamb.

Number 3. Use the common sense that the Lord has given you. Keep your weight normal. Groom yourself attractively. And there is nothing wrong with being in the places where there are eligible Christian males! Mr. Right is on the way, and at the right time, too!

CAN A WIFE BE A MINISTER?

Dear Marilyn:

I feel that I can be honest with you, so I am just going to shoot straight from the hip. I am on your mailing list, and I have noticed that you travel a great deal. How can you minister so much and still be a good wife? How can you be a good mother to your daughter? Surely you don't think that your marriage can withstand such stress. Are you really submissive to your husband?

Dear Friend:

I can certainly understand your questions! To look at my schedule, you can certainly see that it is very busy. However, let me assure you that my husband is very supportive, and I am submissive to him. In fact, if Wally were to tell me to stop traveling tomorrow, I would stop traveling. I know that my husband hears from God, and that he loves me and wants me doing what is best for the kingdom.

I travel because God has led me by His Spirit to travel. In one month I am gone approximately 10 nights, but never more than two or three in a row. When I am gone, I call home several times each day to stay in touch with my family. Of course, if this schedule was not from the Lord, it would definitely strain our family relationship. But I am happy to tell you that I have a very happy marriage and have been married more than 30 years!

My daughter's schedule sometimes seems busier than mine. She is involved in many activities, and I like being a part of them. I like being available to share in her problems, as well as her victories and successes. Again, if I am gone from home, we talk on the telephone and pray together. When I'm at home, Sarah and I spend a good quantity of quality time doing special things together. She is very precious to me, and we have an excellent relationship.

I do not suggest that women start traveling around the countryside to minister unless that is God's specific call. I have never encouraged women to travel this way, and when God calls a married woman to do so, her husband should be in agreement. If any woman has a ministry that her husband

Dear Marilyn

is against, she should take the problem to God. God is "bigger" than husbands, and He can deal with their hearts.

I appreciate your frankness and directness, and I hope that this answers your question.

Dear Marilyn,

Chapter Two
CHILDREN

- **Spanking—Yes or No?**
- **Abusing Privileges at Home**
- **Child With Poor Self-Esteem**
- **Unsaved Children**
- **Child Who Rebels Against Church**

SPANKING—YES OR NO?

Dear Marilyn:

Do you think I am wrong to spank my children? I find disciplining them to be very difficult at times. Spanking seems unloving, especially after I read about the child abuse running rampant in our society. Where does the line stop between spanking and child abuse?

Dear Friend:

The two elements for effective training for your children are love and control. In dealing with your children you need 100% of both of these elements. You cannot control a child whom you don't love, and you cannot love a child whom you don't control. Love and control go hand in hand.

Lamentations 3:27 says, *"It is good for a man that he bear the yoke in his youth."* Discipline benefits our young people and prepares them for responsibility; it does not harm them.

Proverbs 22:6 qualifies the discipline that your children are to receive: *"Train up a child in the way he should go, and when he is old, he will not depart from it."* There is a difference between training and teaching. God wants our children to be trained. What is training? It is the molding of character, instruction by exercise, and drilling by repetition to make our children obedient, to prepare them for maturity, and to point them in one direction. Of course, we are pointing our children in the Lord's direction by instructing them in His ways.

Proverbs 29:15 offers you God's advice when you have to spank your children: *"The rod and reproof give wisdom, but a child left to himself bringeth his mother to shame."* The reason people abuse children is because parents spank in an attitude of anger, which is wrong. Consistency comes in with a parent's realization that bottombeating can never be replaced by browbeating! If it is necessary to spank your child, don't talk about the punishment—talk about the training. Your child won't like it, but Proverbs 19:18 reassures you, *"Chasten your son while there is hope, and let not your soul spare for his crying."*

According to these scriptures, the rod is to be used to correct intentionally wrong actions. Proverbs 22:15 tells you, *"Foolishness is bound in the heart of a child, but the rod of correction will drive it far from him."*

Ask the Lord for discretion as to when spanking is necessary with your child, but you need not confuse it with child abuse. No matter how unique and unusual you think your child is, he still has foolishness in his heart and lacks the ability to think ahead. If you want your child to be free, yet mature enough to make decisions, discipline him by instructing him in God's Word.

When you *do* spank your child, don't forget to forgive him. Tell him how much you love him, and don't ever bring up the incident again. God forgets and so should we. I recommend that before spanking your child, you should pray for him, tell him why he is being spanked, and share what God's Word says about it. Then you will surely be acting in love, not out of anger. Uncontrollable anger was never God's way. God's way is training—not punishment.

To me, however, the best training is preventive: Start speaking God's Word over your child today! Start speaking the Word over yourself as a good parent. Then you can be assured that God will supply you with all the love and wisdom necessary to be the very best parent possible!

ABUSING PRIVILEGES AT HOME

Dear Marilyn:

My husband's 21-year-old son is using our home—or should I say abusing it—as a place to flop when he has nowhere else to go. When he stays at our house, he just mooches everything he can and takes advantage of our hospitality. I am tired of it. This boy has no desire for spiritual things. In fact, he ridicules us about going to church and comments sarcastically about the Bibles and religious reading material in the house. I told my husband that it's time to kick his son out. But then I feel guilty, because I really don't love the boy. What should I do?

Dear Friend:

I was so pleased with your honesty when you said that you didn't feel love for your husband's son. I think that all of us have experienced times when even our own natural children were difficult to handle. Perhaps they were rebellious, so we didn't feel love for them, and then we also felt unspiritual for not loving them.

Once the Lord spoke to me about how to love my own children, and He gave me Mark 12:30: *"Thou shalt love the Lord thy God with all thy heart, and with all thy soul, and with all thy mind, and with all thy strength: this is the first commandment."* I said, "Lord, I know what it is to love you in that way." Then He said, "The second commandment is just like the first one: you shall love your neighbor as you love yourself." Notice that before we can love our neighbors, we have to love God first. Then the Holy Spirit unfolded a revelation that I believe will be of great benefit in your relationship with your husband's son.

When you love the Lord with all your heart, you are focusing your mind and emotions together on loving Him. With all your "strength" stands for God's supernatural strength within. What is God saying? He is saying that whenever, by choice, you begin to sow love in your Heavenly Father, you are also going to reap love. When you begin loving God with all of your being, you suddenly find yourself immersed in His love toward you. That's when you begin to love others with God's love.

How can God's love enter your life and then flow into others in this way? It happens when you begin to love yourself with God's love. You begin to see His image of you—His image that says, "You have a loving nature." You see yourself as important, precious and valuable in His sight. You see yourself as an overcomer. And then you don't just love God and yourself—you also love others with God's love.

Why not spend some time in God's presence and just love Him? Tell Him how much you love Him. Tell God how wonderful He is to you, and let Him saturate you with His love. I believe, as you do so, that you will find a new love—God's love—flowing out to change your stepson's life. Remember, love doesn't fail, but it has to be God's love coming through you.

CHILD WITH POOR SELF-ESTEEM

Dear Marilyn:
My son is a Christian, but he is one of the most defeated people I know. He has very low self-esteem. His skin is acne-prone, he is overweight, has few friends, and is uninterested in extracurricular activities, not even athletics. How can my husband and I encourage our son to have a good self-image?

Children

Dear Friend:

My first suggestion is that you examine the words you speak *to* your son and *about* him. It is essential that your words encourage his development toward having a positive image in Christ—not a negative one in himself.

I remember asking my son, "Why haven't you mowed the lawn yet?"

He answered, "I guess I'm just lazy."

I said, "That is a terrible thing to say about yourself! Don't ever speak that way about yourself again." But then my son asked, "Why not? You say it." His words were like darts piercing my heart. I repented to God and to my son for having contributed to an image of laziness, rather than one of productivity. I vowed never to speak such words again.

Tell your son that he is wise, and make a point to remind him of all his positive attributes. This is to be positive reinforcement, not flattery. But I cannot overemphasize the importance of speaking words of faith to your son and also to God in your prayers. Then continue the process by speaking positively about your son to others.

When the angel of the Lord sought Gideon, he was hiding from the oppressive people of Midian. Gideon was in the severest defeat of his life. He was neither brave nor courageous, yet the angel called out, "Gideon, you are a mighty man of valor! You are going to deliver Israel from the hand of Midian."

It took time for Gideon to see his true image in the Lord. But when the true image sunk in, Gideon led his army to battle, where they all shouted, "The sword of the Lord and of Gideon!" The Lord gave Gideon such self-confidence that the battle cry even contained his name!

As you and your husband begin to speak words of faith over your son, expect transformation. It will thrill you to watch the results that occur. I once read this quote in an article: "Anyone can count the seeds in an apple. But only God can count the apples in a seed."

Imagine the fruitfulness and productivity you will cultivate in your son when, by planting seeds of God's Word, you help your son achieve his full potential in God.

UNSAVED CHILDREN

Dear Marilyn:

I have stood in faith and prayed for my children's salvation for what seems like forever! But they are no better. In fact, my youngest son is now involved in drugs, and I am fearful that he will permanently damage his brain. My daughter has left her husband to live with another man, and she has deserted her children. My prayers seem to have worked in reverse. Can you help me?

Dear Friend:

God can help you. No matter how impossible your children's situations look, don't cast away your confidence. Your faith has great "recompense of reward." The Bible says that in due season we will reap, if we don't faint!

I have an exciting testimony to share with you. It will warm your heart and help you during this trying time. Years ago I went to Albany, New York, for a convention. During one meeting I was strongly led by the Spirit to ask parents to pray for their rebellious children's salvation. After prayer, we sent God's Word to heal those children and deliver them from their destructions. Then I asked the parents to write that evening's date in their Bibles. Thus, when doubts crept in, they could open their Bibles, point to that date, and be firm in their agreement with God's Word.

Years passed, and I had long forgotten the occasion in which the parents prayed for their children at that convention. But one day outside our church, as I greeted people after a service, I was reminded of that convention. A lovely young woman, perhaps in her mid-twenties, walked over to me and said, "I think you should know my story. I moved to Denver six months ago, and I came to your church as a guest. Before I left that day, I had received Jesus Christ as my Lord and Savior and had been baptised with the Holy Spirit.

She continued, "That night I called my parents and told them that I had been born again. Of course, they were ecstatic! They asked which church I had attended, and I said, "Wallace and Marilyn Hickey's church."

The young woman's parents began to weep. They said, "Seven years ago we agreed for your salvation with Marilyn Hickey. We wrote that date of agreement in our Bibles." Their daughter's salvation took seven years before it was manifested. Many heartaches had come during the seven years. But God was faithful to those parents, and He is just as faithful to you.

We cannot cast away our confidence. God is at work, no matter how dark any situation appears. I say to you, "God is bigger than your difficulty." You know it, and I know it, and we are going to stand together for victory. God richly bless you.

CHILD WHO REBELS AGAINST CHURCH

Dear Marilyn:
My son's stubbornness is wearing me down. He is 16 and feels that he is old enough to decide for himself whether he will attend church. Every Sunday morning when the family is getting ready for church, there is a big scene, because my son doesn't want to go. I'm tired of fighting! In fact, my husband and I are ready to give up. Do we have any choice?

Dear Friend:
What challenges teenagers bring to our lives! Or should I say, "What opportunities to believe God for miracles." I am sure that you're spending time praying for your son, because that is your number-one weapon for this spiritual battle. Secondly, have you considered offering him some incentive for attending church? Think of something that your son enjoys, and make it a reward for attending church. You can begin talking about that reward early in the week—Monday isn't too soon! Help your son with his own mental preparation for church, so that you won't have these head-on confrontations. You need the mental preparation as much as he does.

If your son refuses to attend church, perhaps you should restrict some of his weekly activities. If he does attend church, you might even take him out to lunch for a heart-to-heart talk. Discuss his reasons for not wanting to go to church. Talk about them in a manner that won't put him on the defensive. Pray with him (don't prey on him), and make sure he knows that you love him unconditionally—no matter what he does!

My final suggestion is that you check your own

conversation. Do you criticize the church, its leadership, or those who attend? If so, repent and stop speaking negatively. Even if your conversation has been innocent of criticism, make an extra effort to cultivate a conversation that will plant positive thoughts about church in your son. God wants to help us with our teenagers. If we are sensitive to His voice, we will be the winners and so will our children.

Dear Marilyn,

Chapter Three
FRIENDS AND RELATIVES

- Unsaved Relatives
- Ridicule by Unsaved Family
- Friends in False Doctrine
- Possessive In-laws
- Death of Unsaved Loved One

UNSAVED RELATIVES

Dear Marilyn:
I have close relatives who are aware of my stand for the Lord. The problem is that they invent every possible excuse for rejecting salvation. Either they prefer a traditional doctrine that doesn't embrace salvation, or they say, "It's too difficult for me to change." Can I pray for God to change my relatives' wills?

Dear Friend:
Very often your prayers will go against natural circumstances! For example, you may pray for a marriage to succeed, even after one partner has given up. You may pray for rebellious children. And certainly you may pray for the salvation of your unsaved relatives. Does God override another person's free will? Can we pray that God will change someone's will? I believe that we can.

God has chosen to work through believers ever since Jesus first redeemed us. Jesus rose from the dead, was given a name above all names, was seated by God's right hand, and received all authority. After receiving that authority, Jesus came to Christians and said, "I give you all power." We have His "power of attorney" to use on earth. God has given us the same authority as Jesus. Why? So that on earth we can accomplish God's will, including the salvation of unsaved people.

Our responsibility as Christians is outlined in the scriptures. Matthew 16:19b says, *"Whatsoever thou shalt bind on earth shall be bound in heaven: and whatsoever thou shalt loose on earth shall be loosed in heaven."* I believe that we are to bind the devil's work and loose God's work in the lives of unbelievers.

God also wants us to pray for the lost in Jesus' name: *"And whatsoever ye shall ask in my name, that will I do, that the Father may be glorified in the Son. If ye shall ask any thing in my name, I will do it"* (John 14:13,14).

Another scripture revealing God's will for your unsaved relatives is 1 John 5:14,15: *"If we ask any thing according to his will, he heareth us: And if we know that he hear us, whatsoever we ask, we know that we have the petitions that we desired of him"* (1 John 5:14b,15).

Is it God's will to save your relatives? Yes, it is! God hears your prayers and grants them when they are in line with His will. Matthew 9:29 confirms, *"According to your faith, be it unto you."* Matthew 21:22 says, *"All things whatsoever ye shall ask in prayer, believing, ye shall receive."* Your prayers of faith are the key to unlock salvation for those whom you love.

God wants to reunite marriages. He wants to save rebellious people, and He wants to transform their lives. Many times we try to fight these situations with our human, emotional, and psychological weapons. But such weapons can never win spiritual battles! God only answers prayer according to His Word, so let's purpose to pray that way.

Here are some scriptures we can pray for unsaved people. Psalm 68:18 says, *"Thou hast received gifts for men; yea, for the rebellious also, that the Lord God might dwell among them."* Proverbs 21:1 is for leaders: *"The king's heart is in the hand of the Lord, as the rivers of water: he turneth it whithersoever he will."*

God changed your will. Every time you look in the mirror you see a person whose will was turned around by God. Therefore, God can change the wills of others. Bind the devil's work and loose God's work in your relatives' lives. Ask for their salvation in the name of Jesus. God's Word won't return void!

RIDICULE BY UNSAVED FAMILY

Dear Marilyn:

I'm the only one in my family who is saved, and I really feel alone. Whenever we have family gatherings, I am always the focus for very unkind remarks and negative comments that really hurt. Some of my relatives refer to me as "holier than thou" or "the holy roller." I have a deep desire to see my loved ones become saved, so I cannot run from the situation. How can I handle this with wisdom and love?

Dear Friend:

Be very encouraged! Psalm 68:6 says, *"God setteth the solitary in families; he bringeth out those who are bound wtih chains."* You have been placed in your family to bring your unsaved loved ones into Christ's freedom!

There is a special promise in 1 Peter 4:14 for you to claim during these family times when you suffer verbal persecution: *"If ye be reproached for the name of Christ, happy are ye: for the Spirit of glory and of God resteth upon you; on their part he is evil spoken of, but on your part he is glorified."* God's glory is going to shine radiantly through you for two purposes: first, to make you strong; and second, to make you a light for your family.

The Lord's light shining from your heart is far greater than any darkness that is in your family. God promised that the path of the just would shine more brightly unto the Lord's coming (Proverbs 4:18). Begin praying that your light will shine so brightly that your family can no longer be blinded to the truth, but that the veil over their eyes will be lifted and they will receive the Lord.

When God told Abraham that the cities of Sodom and Gomorrah would be destroyed because of the people's sins, Abraham prayed and interceded for Lot and his family. When the appointed time for destruction came, God remembered Abraham's prayers. Lot and his family were spared.

The Bible doesn't tell you, "God remembered Lot." It says that God remembered Abraham who prayed for Lot's family. Pray for your loved ones, and God will remember those prayers and answer them. Your prayers of faith are powerful, so don't be discouraged. Hold fast to them, and the wall of darkness in your family will crumble, light will break through, and your loved ones will enter the family of God!

FRIENDS IN FALSE DOCTRINE

Dear Marilyn:

I am writing to you about some friends of mine who are involved in false doctrine. They are so deceived that they actually do not believe that heaven or hell are literal places. These friends, however, claim that their beliefs are validated in the Bible. Now they are harrassing me to believe as they do. How can I talk to these people?

Dear Friend:

Don't give up on your friends! If you cannot speak to them

or give them literature, then I have an excellent scripture that you can pray on their behalf. It is Isaiah 29:24, *"They also that erred in spirit shall come to understanding, and they that murmured shall learn doctrine."*

Your friends have erred. But you can pray this promise for them to return to right understanding. Once a group of young men who were involved with false prophecy started coming to our church. One of the men prophesied over another young man. The man prophesying said, "Give away your wealth, hitchhike to Jerusalem, and live on a kibbutz." My husband and I had no idea that this was going on, of course. The man who received the prophecy was very wealthy, and guess who was given his money? The man who had made the false prophecy.

All of this happened secretly. My husband and I did not discover the incident until the deceived young man was on his way to New York City. My husband and I called in the other man, who had given the false prophecy, and rebuked him sharply. As a result, he left our church.

My husband and I immediately began to claim Isaiah 29:24 for the young man who had been deceived. He stayed in Israel for several months and then returned to Denver. We saw him at a restaurant one day, and he treated us very coldly. But we did not give up. I don't believe in giving up, because God wants us to pray until we win! The game wasn't over. We had not yet won. We kept on believing and speaking the Word that, although the young man had "erred in spirit," he would come to right understanding.

Almost a year later my husband met the young man at a Full Gospel Businessmen's convention. The man apologized and said, "I know that you really cared and wanted me to see the truth. I was so deceived. Thank you for praying." Today that man is serving God wholeheartedly.

Don't give up on your friends. Don't listen to their doctrines or argue with them. Just keep on praying in the authority of God's Word. Ask God to enlighten the eyes of your friends' understanding...and He will!

POSSESSIVE IN-LAWS

Dear Marilyn:

You always seem to be able to answer practical, down-to-earth questions, so I've got one for you. How do I deal with my in-laws? They are so possessive about the time that we spend with them! Their possessiveness is about to drive me crazy. They want us to spend every holiday with them: Christmas, Thanksgiving, Easter, Memorial Day—you name it! Our family never gets to spend those special occasions with our own choice of friends, or just be alone together. I don't want to offend my in-laws, but I'm tired of the way they have needed to call the shots.

Dear Friend:

Sometimes it seems as though our in-laws become "outlaws!" It's especially difficult when they are demanding great amounts of our personal time. Your question made me want to look at some Biblical examples of good in-laws, and then at some bad ones.

Naomi was an excellent mother-in-law who introduced her Moabite daughter-in-law to the living God. Ruth became a marvelous daughter, who is now in the lineage of Jesus! Another example of a wonderful in-law was Jephthah, Moses' generous father-in-law, whose wise counsel helped govern thousands of people. Actually, Jephthah treated

Moses more kindly than did Moses' own wife!

Then there were the negative examples of in-laws. Laban was one of them. He was Jacob's scheming father-in-law, and Jacob desperately needed some distance from him. God arranged for that distance, and Jacob took Rachel and Leah back to his original home. I am not suggesting that you physically move away from your in-laws. However, there are other ways to create the distance you need.

Your first step is to pray and forgive your in-laws. Ask God for wisdom and love to deal with the situation at hand, and then start planning for the next major holiday—approximately six months in advance.

Begin immediately to prepare your in-laws for a change in plans for the next holiday. Give them space to make other plans for themselves in preparing for that change. Most importantly, love them, love them, love them. Send flowers and write a note expressing how much you appreciate them.

There is a fourth step that should permeate every aspect of the change you are making for your holidays: Remember to trust God in every aspect of this situation. Don't examine the problem and dig out the past. Leave it with God. This is not your problem any longer. Give it to God and He will smooth it out.

DEATH OF UNSAVED LOVED ONES

Dear Marilyn:
I am almost sick with grief over my father's recent death. I am not sure whether he was a Christian, so I don't know whether he went to heaven. Sometimes I feel resentful toward God. I almost don't care whether I personally go to heaven if

my father won't be there. How can I deal with this mental and emotional suffering?

Dear Friend:
Unfortunately, there are difficult times for all of us when our loved ones die—whether saved or not. But when we are unsure of a person's salvation, that person's death can hurt us deeply. Although you may be unsure about your father's salvation, I am sure that you prayed for him. Now trust God that His Word was performed. Don't lean to your own understanding—your sense knowledge—any longer.

I faced a similar situation when my own father died. In the time directly following his death, I made a decision to believe that the seed of God's Word in my father's heart did not return void. One of my family members, however, was almost suffocating in grief. Her sorrow was so deep that I was concerned about her physical health. I prayed about her, and the Holy Spirit gave me the key to unlock this loved one's sorrow. He showed me that Jesus carried our sins, sicknesses, and griefs. Then I saw that this relative was not allowing Jesus to carry her grief. She was carrying it alone.

I called the loved one and ministered God's Word to her. When she realized that the Lord wanted to deliver her from grief, she cast her sorrows on Jesus and was set free. Today God is using her in the ministry.

Now let me ask you, "Have you cast your burden of grief on the Lord?" Grief can give you a nervous breakdown. It can physically harm you, and you were not designed to carry it. Right now, cast your sorrows on Jesus. He said, *"Come to me, all ye that labour and are heavy laden, and I will give you rest"* (Matthew 11:28).

Repent of your bitterness. Let Jesus carry your grief and

bring the rest and refreshing of the Holy Spirit to your soul. You will find that the joy of the Lord is truly your strength.

Dear Marilyn,

Chapter Four
SEX

- **Virginity—Old Fashioned?**
- **Living in Sin**
- **Adultery—Just Once?**
- **Unclean Thoughts**
- **Improper Teacher–Student Relationship**

VIRGINITY—OLD FASHIONED?

Dear Marilyn:

Don't you think that in our day virginity is old-fashioned? I heard a minister state that marriage will be outmoded in the next 10 years. Almost every television program, magazine, and movie that I see encourages free-swinging sex. I used to believe that both men and women should be virgins when they marry, but now I am beginning to think that this view is unrealistic. Do you think that Christians should change with the times?

Dear Friend:

In the Bible marriage is compared to the relationship Jesus has with His people. God uses the image of marriage fidelity to describe His faithfulness to us and His people's faithfulness to Him. When you read the Old Testament, you find that polygamy is tolerated—a man could have more than one wife. But this is far from God's original plan, which had one man with one woman.

However, I have never seen God tolerate premarital sex. The Bible never speaks of people living together and having sexual relationships before they are married. The only sexual acts found outside of marriage in the Bible are prostitution, rape, and adultery.

I like the fact that the Bible is very gut-level and tells things like they really are. David had a son who was extremely attracted to his half-sister Tamar. He tricked her into his bedroom and forced her into sexual relations with him. Afterwards he hated her with as much strength as he had desired her before. It is a tragic story and the whole episode ends with murder.

Jacob's only daughter, Dinah, was raped by a Hivite when he came into the Promised Land. This story ends up with Jacob's sons killing the Hivites. All we see is tragedy!

Sex is good and meant to be enjoyed. But God also made sexual relationships sacred and to be shared only in marriage. Nowhere in the Bible does God give a double standard. Virginity is very much "in-style" today, just as it was in Genesis. We do not change the rules as time goes by.

You are not an oddball for being a virgin. You are a born-again believer. You are to be more than a conqueror on this earth. Many young people are floundering from the lack of an ethical standard and are told to do their "own thing." But my husband and I have pastored one church for 24 years, and we have seen the psychological scars that are left from illicit sexual relationships. Everyone should keep himself or herself for his or her own spouse. Christians don't change with the times. They change the times with God's Word.

LIVING IN SIN

Dear Marilyn:
My son is living with a girl without being married to her. Both of them are unsaved, but I did not raise my son to live this way. I feel hurt because he knows better. The girl, however, comes from a bad background. I think that her mother lives in a fashion similar to that of her daughter. I like the girl and I don't want to cut off communication with my son, but I want them to be saved and get married, instead of living in sin. How shall I treat them? How should I handle holidays and dinners when they are present? I want to be a Christian, but I do not want to condone sin.

Dear Friend:

Sometimes it can be so difficult to make spiritual decisions. Certainly in situations such as yours we need the Lord's own wisdom. In 1 Corinthians 1:30 you are told that Jesus is made unto you wisdom; and 1 Corinthians 2:16 says that you have the mind of Christ. First of all, you should claim the wisdom of Jesus for your situation, and secondly, you should express the Lord's love toward your son and his girlfriend.

I do not suggest that you allow your son and his girlfriend to sleep in the same room when they are at your house. That would be condoning their sin. However, welcome them to visit on holidays and other occasions. If you cut off communication with your son, then you will lose the opportunity to share the Word with him as the Lord permits. Your son and his girlfriend need to be around someone who will influence them spiritually. Then conviction—not condemnation—can enter in and make them want Jesus in their lives. Condemnation always fails. But love **never** fails.

When the Holy Spirit opens the door, be honest with your son. He probably knows your feelings anyway. If you are honest and positive and share what God wants to do in these two young lives, they will be receptive. Don't play up the problem. Playing up a problem will only enlarge it. I suggest that you play it down and pray it up! Spend a great deal of time praying, but when you are around your son and his girlfriend, do not act as though their lifestyle is a problem. God bless you as you walk in His wisdom for your situation.

ADULTERY—JUST ONCE?

Dear Marilyn:

I never dreamed that I would write this letter. The thing

that I thought "only happened to others" is actually happening to me. I am a Christian who is married and has two wonderful children. But I am starting to feel attracted to a very handsome man in my office. He keeps taking me to coffee for break time. Now he has asked me to go out to dinner with him some evening after work. I am very tempted. This man is not a Christian, but he is very kind. I cannot help thinking that "just once" won't hurt anything, but this attraction disturbs me.

Dear Friend:
You are asking, pleading, and begging for big trouble. Not only do I suggest that you break the dinner invitation, I also recommend that you don't even take breaks with the man. Above **all**, don't go out with him. From reading your letter, I am sure that the reason you wrote to me is because you already know the answer in your heart.

There is one emergency exit for you. You must state emphatically out of your mouth to this man, "NO! No more coffee breaks, no dinner, nothing." You may say, "It has been innocent this far." But the Bible commands Christians to shun the very appearance of evil. We are to flee from temptation. You can flee from temptation in these three ways:

1. Look ahead. Sit down and write out the consequences that could come from an involvement with this man. Is the risk of losing your family worth it? Do you want to reap what you sow?

2. Look around. You have a good marriage, good children, good health, a good job, and a wonderful Lord. God has given you so many things. Why would you stop the flow of His goodness by inviting temptation and sin?

3. **Look within.** He who is in you is greater than the enemy who is prowling about with temptation. God, who dwells in you by the Holy Spirit, gives you supernatural ability to say "No," to sin and "Yes," to grace, mercy and love.

I know that as you look ahead to judgment, around to God's goodness, and within to Christ's ability, you will gain the necessary strength to make a righteous decision.

UNCLEAN THOUGHTS

Dear Marilyn:

What's wrong with me? I love the Lord and want very much to serve Him wholeheartedly, yet my carnal mind gets in the way. Of course, I don't want to have bad or unclean thoughts, but I have them anyway. Sometimes I even have dreams that I know would be displeasing to God. I feel terrible about all of this, yet I don't know how to control my mind.

Dear Friend:

The Bible has a lot to say about how God's people can bring "uncontrollable minds" into submission to the Word. For one thing, God has told us that we are to "pull down strongholds, cast down imaginations, and bring every thought into the obedience of Christ" (2 Corinthians 10:4b,5a). You **can** bring your thoughts into the obedience of Christ!

The devil has tried to influence your mind in this fashion: first, he brings in a thought; as you consider it, the thought becomes an imagination; and when you imagine it, then it has a stronghold in your thought patterns. What you must do now is pull down those strongholds with God's Word.

Start by asking the Holy Spirit to show you from where these unclean thoughts first came. Then speak aloud to those thoughts. Tell them to come under obedience to the mind of Christ. In addition to any other scriptures the Lord gives you, claim the mind of Christ for yourself. This is how you begin to pull down a stronghold. But not only are you pulling it down, you are also building a new stronghold of God's Word.

As God's Word becomes a stronghold in your mind, you will start thinking according to the mind of Christ by the Holy Spirit within you. I have often spoken the Word to my mind, so I know that this works. I say, "Mind, you will think the thoughts of Christ!"

If the devil keeps harassing my mind, I continue with spiritual warfare by repeating memorized scripture. This is a tremendous way to cleanse your mind: it's the washing of the water by the Word! Try meditating on scripture, and the devil won't dare torment your mind! Instead, the Word will renew your mind.

It's exciting to think that we can replace evil thoughts with righteous ones. Stop being in defeat! You do not have to possess a carnal, defeated mind. You were given the mind of Christ to USE in these times!

IMPROPER TEACHER—STUDENT RELATIONSHIPS

Dear Marilyn:
Recently one of my son's teachers has initiated a close friendship with my son. Suddenly he is receiving great kindness and interest from this teacher, but I am concerned

that the attention is too much. This teacher even writes notes to my son and calls him. Isn't this strange conduct for a teacher to have toward a student?

Dear Friend:
A problem similar to yours arose for some people who attend our church. In this case, however, the teacher was a woman paying excessive attention to one of her students. The teacher was very athletically inclined, as was the student, so this was a basis of appeal. As in your son's case, the student was receiving telephone calls and notes from the teacher. They even attended a few movies and sports events together. Just as you are concerned, the girl's mother was quite disturbed by the situation, yet she couldn't pinpoint the reason why.

Finally the girl's mother called me and discussed the situation in brief detail. She told me that she was concerned that the relationship was unprofessional on the part of the teacher. We prayed and asked the Holy Spirit to reveal the truth, because the Holy Spirit is the Spirit of truth. The very next morning the mother had her answer.

After the daughter had gone to school, her mother received a telephone call from a woman who informed her that this teacher had been involved in a lesbian relationship during her college years. The mother knew that this was the answer, and she shared it with her daughter that afternoon. Of course, the girl was crushed, since she was very flattered by the special attention. But she was immediately concerned that people would think she was a lesbian. She had previously wondered why the teacher had been focusing interest on her. Only through prayer and assurance from God's Word were that girl's emotions restored. This whole situation could have been disastrous if the girl's mother had not been quick to watch, pray, and listen to the guidance of the Holy Spirit.

I strongly advise you to ask the Holy Spirit to show you the truth about this situation, whether through circumstances or an inner witness—or both. If necessary, you might call the principal of your son's school and advise him on the situation. Ask him whether he considers this behavior to be professional on the part of an employee. School systems are particularly concerned with problems of this nature. My advice is that you deal with the situation immediately, with God's help.

Dear Marilyn,

Chapter Five
PERSONAL PROBLEMS

- **Unholy Temper**
- **Quitting Smoking**
- **Bad Influences from Others**
- **Weight Control**
- **Self-Condemnation**
- **Overcoming Putdowns**

Personal Problems

UNHOLY TEMPER

Dear Marilyn:

My wife thinks that I have a very quick temper. I guess that I do. But when I read the Bible, I find out that Jesus had a temper, and He would become angry on occasion. I don't think all anger is sin, yet I don't want to be undisciplined in this area of my life. I especially don't want to have my wife nagging me all the time about my hot temper, and I don't want to frighten my children. Please, can you help me?

Dear Friend:

Maybe you have heard this before—if you are angry at someone, count to 10 before saying anything. But recently I read something that is so much better. If you are really angry, then before speaking, count to nine by naming the fruits of the Spirit. They are found in Galatians 5:22,23: Love, joy, peace, long-suffering, gentleness, goodness, faith, meekness, and temperance. Memorize them! They will help.

Yes, Jesus did lose his temper. There is no question that He became angry when He had healed on the Sabbath day and the Pharisees had accused Him of wrongdoing. The Bible says that Jesus was *"grieved for the hardness of their hearts"* (Mark 3:5). Jesus looked into their souls, and He became angry with Satan's working within these men's hearts.

Another situation where Jesus expressed anger was when the priest and scribes made a large profit from sacrificial animals in the temple. He dumped over the tables and chased out men (Matthew 21:12,13). Jesus was angry with the enemy and his co-workers.

The difference between Jesus' anger and carnal anger is that Jesus didn't get angry over wrongs done to Himself.

Because Christ was always in control of Himself, He never lost his temper in a carnal way. He knew exactly what He was doing at all times. We lose our temper because we are out of control. When Jesus was badly treated, he responded with gentleness and love. He prayed to the Father that He would forgive those who were crucifying Him.

Certainly anger can bring sin. Paul wrote in Ephesians 4:26,27, *"Be ye angry, and sin not; let not the sun go down upon your wrath; Neither give place to the devil."* So anger can either bring sin or be without sin. It depends on our motives. Are we angry at the devil for what he is doing? Or are we angry and just bad-tempered because we have been mishandled?

Let me give you a few quick pointers that I feel will be helpful to you. Number one, before you get out of bed every morning, pray Psalms 141:3, *"Set a watch, O Lord, before my mouth; keep the door of my lips."*

Number two, when you are angry count the nine fruits of the Spirit before saying a word.

Number three, pray in the Holy Spirit.

I believe these three steps will help you cool down your temper. God will help you speak honestly without anger. I thank the Lord for your honesty and your sincere desire for change in your life.

QUITTING SMOKING

Dear Marilyn:
I am writing because, after smoking cigarettes for 20 years, I cannot quit. I have tried to quit smoking so many times that I can't count them. I am a born-again Christian, who really

loves the Lord, but I cannot seem to stop smoking. What should I do?

Dear Friend:
I can confidently assure you that God is stronger than any habit you have. Literally thousands of people have been permanently delivered from smoking cigarettes through a scriptural remedy that I have set forth at conventions and through radio and television.

The people who have been set free from smoking cigarettes have put their faith in Luke 10:9, *"Behold, I give unto your power to tread on serpents and scorpions, and over all the power of the enemy."*

Right now, take your pack(s) of cigarettes, and throw them on the floor with your matches and lighter. Start saying the scripture I just gave you. As you stomp those cigarettes under your feet, say, "I have been given power to tread on serpents and scorpions, and over all the power of the enemy!"

By doing this, you have spoken and acted in faith on God's Word. The Bible says that God sets you free from the things upon which you tread, so you have been set free from smoking cigarettes. They cannot have power over you any longer.

I have a final scripture for you: *"If the Son therefore shall make you free ye shall be free indeed"* (John 8:36). You may have to speak God's Word many times every day initially to retain your freedom. But if you keep speaking the Word, just as Jesus said, "It is written," to the devil, you will never be in bondage to cigarettes again! Any desire to smoke will leave forever. I want to hear about your victory. This has worked for others, and I know that it will work for you.

BAD INFLUENCES FROM OTHERS

Dear Marilyn:
I feel as though I am the weakest Christian in the world. Just when things seem fine, I fall in line with the wrong crowd. Then suddenly I'm involved in gossip, dirty jokes, and everything else I want to avoid. I can't get away from these people because I work with them every day. I haven't made my stand as a Christian, although I wish that I could. How can I avoid this frustrating trap?

Dear Friend:
It is certainly true that we conduct ourselves like those around whom we spend time. I remember the story where Henny Penny ran through the barnyard clucking, "The sky is falling! The sky is falling!" Soon all the animals in the barnyard did the same thing. Likewise, we can spend our time with Henny-Pennies and begin acting just like them.

The "sky has been falling" in worldly situations for thousands of years. It's nothing new. But if we Christians fly with the eagles—as God intended—then we'll escape the barnyard and soar in the Spirit. Then no matter what happens around us, we can live according to our supernatural God, with whom we spend our time.

You have a decision to make. If you choose to be around Henny Pennies, then before long the sky won't be falling—you'll be falling. I recommend that you choose to fly with the eagles. Spend your time with mature Christians, who can influence you in your walk with the Lord. You may have to seek them out, but soon other Henny-Pennies will seek **you** out, because you will be soaring.

When I read about young David, the giant-killer, I saw that

Personal Problems

he didn't consider his situation as one of being personally faced with a giant. Instead, David said, "That giant is coming against God." Knowing that God wouldn't let His people down, David was able to win over the giant. First, David prepared mentally. He rehearsed aloud his past victories in God. Then David advanced and killed the giant. Because of that act, David was a popular man in Israel—so popular that the king of Israel resolved to take David's life. David fled and ended up alone in a cave.

Soon afterward, God sent David 600 men who had all been misfits in some way. But what happened when those men met David? They became giant killers, too! The next group of men who killed giants in the Bible was all David's men. Men who were misfits were changed and transformed because they chose to be with David, a man after God's own heart.

You may not always be able to choose the people with whom you spend time. But if I were you, I would start being involved with every Christian available. I would saturate myself in God's Word and pray in the Spirit a great deal. By doing this, **you** will be the giant killer. Don't let Henny Pennies change you. Instead, change them!

WEIGHT CONTROL

Dear Marilyn:

I have been heavy since I was a teenager, and now that I am middle-aged, I have a terrible time controlling my weight. I have even wondered if I might have a spirit of lust for food! There must be a scriptural answer to help me. Can you please tell me how to solve this problem?

Dear Friend:

I want to give you five simple ways to apply God's Word to

your life. If you do these things, you will be set free from an excessive appetite. First of all, 1 Corinthians 10:31 tells you, *"Whether therefore ye eat, or drink, or whatsoever ye do, do all to the glory of God."* Before you even step out of bed in the morning, give your appetite to God. Say, "Whatever I eat today will bring You glory." As you speak those words, your appetite will be placed under God's control.

Second, remember that having an idle mind will make you hungry. Proverbs 19:15 says, *"Slothfulness casteth into a deep sleep, and an idle soul shall suffer hunger."* Keep your mind fastened on God's Word, and keep your mind active. Get the tapes of the New Testament and play them whenever you have a chance. You can even play the tapes in your car!

My third recommendation is that you ask God to help you take authority over wrong eating habits. The Bible is your source for recognizing what is wrong and what is all right. Proverbs 23:3 says, *"Be not desirous of his dainties, for they are deceitful meat."* Foods that are high in fats and calories, and low in nutrition—such as bakery goodies—are deceitful meat. They look attractive, but they are bad for your physical health. Proverbs 23:2 tells you how to take authority over them: *"Put a knife to your throat if you be a man given to appetite."* What is that knife? It's the sword of God's Word! It will put your spirit in control of your flesh.

Number four, you should pray in the Spirit whenever possible. Romans 8:26 tells you why: *"Likewise the Spirit also helpeth our infirmities. For we know not what we should pray for as we ought; but the Spirit itself maketh intercession for us with groanings that cannot be uttered."* The Holy Spirit is your helper. He will deliver you from your weakness for food if you will pray in the Spirit.

Fifth, ask God to feed you according to Proverbs 30:8b:

"Feed me with food convenient for me." A gluttonous appetite is out of control. But an appetite that belongs to God is **under** control, and glorifies Him. There is **no** question that you will lose weight by applying these principles to your life. Focus on God's Word rather than food. Your appetite will be placed in divine order!

SELF-CONDEMNATION

Dear Marilyn:

Every time I make a mistake in my walk with God, I go over that failure again and again in my mind. Then I wonder if I am actually saved. I know that the Bible says that I'm saved and I should not condemn myself. But how can I change those thoughts?

Dear Friend:

God's Word can take away condemnation and bring you transformation. Your struggle with feelings of condemnation reminds me of something that happened when my husband and I vacationed in New Mexico. When we were driving through the beautiful, high mountain plains surrounding Santa Fe, I noticed some very unusual buildings. They looked like churches because there were crosses on them. But there were no windows on these buildings. When I mentioned this to my husband, he said, "Marilyn, those buildings are called *moradas* or 'houses of death.' The people who attend those churches are called *penitentes* and they actually beat themselves to try to draw closer to God. During Easter those people will even crucify someone if they can get away with it."

I was horrified by the very idea of a person thinking that

beating himself on the outside could make him closer to God on the inside. But then the Lord spoke to me, "Marilyn, many Christians wouldn't dream of beating themselves on the outside, but many of them beat themselves on the inside." You are doing exactly that by condemning yourself.

You need to have a heart-to-heart talk with your own heart. Speak the Word of God in order to turn aside thoughts of condemnation: *"For if our heart condemn us, God is greater than our heart and knoweth all things. Beloved if our heart condemn us not, then we have confidence toward God"* (1 John 3:20,21).

Repent of having condemned yourself, because God has forgiven you. In 1 John 1:9 it says, *"If we confess our sins, he is faithful and just to forgive us our sins, and to cleanse us from all unrighteousness."* Say aloud, "Heart, you cannot condemn me anymore. I have been forgiven and cleansed from sin."

Jesus' precious blood was shed so that you could walk in confidence toward God. Walk, talk, and act the Lord's righteousness in you. Don't depend on your own righteousness. You have the righteousness of Jesus, which is more than enough! God's Son set you free, so you have a right to walk in His freedom.

OVERCOMING PUTDOWNS

Dear Marilyn:
I am 16 years old and a Christian. My problem is that my older sister is always putting me down, even though she is also a Christian. When I talk about the things in which I believe, she puts me down. She doesn't realize that I have

spiritual dreams just like she does. Sometimes I talk to my parents and receive encouragement, but they don't know what my sister is doing. What can I do about her put-downs?

Dear Friend:

Jesus said that offenses will come. Even though offenses are unpleasant, they are still present. Not only will we be offended by others, but we will be guilty of offending others. Yet God said that we are blessed when we aren't offended in Him. The best way to overcome those feelings of hurt is to remember that you are in Christ.

In 1 Samuel 17 David brought food to his brothers. When he arrived with the food, a giant named Goliath came out to challenge Israel's armies. When David heard the challenge, his heart leaped! He wanted to help, but his older brother said, "What can you do? You're just a shepherd, so go on home."

Instead of being hurt, David continued to be concerned deeply for the cause of God and His people. Instead of being "put down," David, in the power of the Lord, went out and killed Goliath. The Philistine army was defeated because of one young man's faith! What I want you to see is that David did not allow his older brother's offense to be a distraction.

Offenses are the devil's deliberate traps meant to keep us from killing giants in our own lives. But God has given us the weapon of His Word and the power of His Holy Spirit. Stay in Jesus and hold fast to His Word to keep your goals. Remember that any adversity to your God-given goals is from the devil. I know that you won't give up because you are going to make a resolution in Jesus not to be taken in by the devil's traps.

Dear Marilyn,

Chapter Six
THE BIBLE

- **Which Bible Translation Should I Read?**
- **Bible Reading Consistency?**
- **When is the Tribulation?**
- **Spirit, Soul, and Body—Which is Which?**
- **Is Loud Prayer Scriptural?**

WHICH BIBLE TRANSLATION SHOULD I READ?

Dear Marilyn:

I am a new Christian who has difficulty reading the Bible and understanding it. I do understand, however, that for me to grow, I must start reading my Bible every day. I want to be committed, but I have been told that the only right version is the King James Version—the most difficult translation for me to understand! Other people have told me to read the Living Bible. It's much simpler, but I want to be doing what is right. What do you suggest?

Dear Friend:

First of all, I'm thrilled with your determination to stick with God's Word. A foundation in the Word is the best thing you can build for a strong future.

Personally, I believe that different translations of the Bible meet different needs. I love the King James Bible, but perhaps that is partly because I have done so much memorization from that version. I have also been reading from the King James since I was 11 years old. Another reason I use it, read it, and teach from it is because it seems to be the most commonly-used Bible.

My husband, however, prefers the New International Version of the Bible because it is very clear. I agree with him, the NIV is an excellent translation. But I still keep returning to the King James.

Frances Hunter has encouraged me for years to read the Living Bible, a paraphrased version. She feels that it unfolds the Bible's complexities and makes the Word come alive. I know that the Living Bible is enjoyed by brand new and mature Christians alike!

I don't think you should worry about what other people tell you to read. I recommend that you go to a Bible bookstore with a good selection of Bibles. Plan to spend an hour just browsing and comparing translations to find the one that you prefer and the one you feel will feed your soul in the best way.

The main thing I want to stress is that you purpose in your heart to read the Bible every day. Beginning with the New Testament, read at least two or three chapters. Keep a red pencil by your side to underline special passages of scripture that the Holy Spirit illuminates to you.

It is also beneficial to read your Bible early in the morning. Your mind is fresh, open, and seems to be more easily renewed with the Word. Many times I have found that my early-morning scriptures apply to my whole day! May God richly bless you as you spend time in His Word every day. All of us are winners when we commit ourselves to the Word—no matter what translation we read!

BIBLE READING CONSISTENCY?

Dear Marilyn:
I have difficulty reading my Bible consistently. I will read it every day for a week, and then when something comes up I won't read my Bible for two to three weeks. I feel so guilty that finally I pick it up again, but I am never consistent. I feel like an up-and-down Christian although that is not my heart's desire. What's wrong with me? Can you help?

Dear Friend:
I know that I can help you. Through the power of God I

have helped thousands and thousands of people get into a consistent daily Bible-reading plan. Perhaps you have been setting your goals too high, or perhaps you did not have any goals with which to work. If your goals are too high then you may reach them for a while and then drop them. But without goals you have nothing to attain.

I suggest that you take three chapters of your Bible each day and five chapters on Sunday. In one year you will totally finish your Bible. Reading three chapters each day only takes about 15 or 20 minutes, and that is not much time. But that little amount of time will make a big difference in your life. On the topic of inconsistency, I understand that it takes 21 days to make a habit. If you will set aside 21 days to read three chapters of your Bible every morning and five on Sunday mornings, you will get hooked on a daily reading plan. I have found that the pattern is so strong that you wouldn't think of missing it! You will have a Bible habit.

Don't start with a huge amount; start small and build as the Lord leads you. When you are consistent with a small amount, God does big things.

Ask God to give you revelation knowledge from His Word each day. Sometimes when I read my Bible it doesn't seem that I am benefiting. But the Lord showed me something very special. He reminded me of the time when I was a child in the Texas panhandle, and my mother would ask me to help her can peaches. I didn't like the work, and the kitchen was hot and uncomfortable. But we never complained in the winter when we opened jars of peaches and ate that delicious fruit. God's Word can be that way, too. It may seem tedious (for a while), to read His Word, but you are "canning" the Word in your heart for the wintery seasons of your life. When they come, God brings His Word from your heart and makes it wisdom in your life.

Psalm 51:6 says, *"Thou desirest truth in the inward parts: and in the hidden part thou shalt make me to know wisdom."* God wants you to hide truth in your heart so that He can make it wisdom for your daily life. Begin small and God will honor your daily commitment. It will work for you—I know it will.

WHEN IS THE TRIBULATION?

Dear Marilyn:

I have some very dear friends who believe that Christians are going to suffer through the tribulation on earth. They believe that the rapture will come after the tribulation. Their beliefs put fear in my heart, and the thought of enduring the tribulation really upsets me. I have some other friends who say that Christians will only endure half of the tribulation and then be raptured. I personally believe that Jesus will take us from the earth beforehand. How shall I deal with Christians who disagree with me about the timing of the rapture?

Dear Friend:

There is much discussion in our day regarding the pre-, mid-, and post-tribulation raptures. I have no quarrel with any person studying God's Word and discussing when the rapture will occur. But what is important to me is that the subject should not be divisive to the Body of Christ. The devil wants to divide Christians on such subjects, and we must stand against that division.

One thing I do know is that Christians are to be ready for the moment when Jesus comes back for us. Whether before, in the middle, or after the tribulation, our hearts and lives are supposed to line up with God's Word. It is very important that we are looking for the return of Christ by walking in holiness and walking in love.

It seems to me that today some Christians want to make up the rules of Christianity as they go. I don't believe that this is a good preparation for Christ's return. We all want to be winners, but a Christian can't win while living in sin. We need to watch our lives diligently and daily. We need to be repentant of sin and ask God to purge us from it so that we can walk in the power of the Holy Spirit. Then, when Jesus comes, we'll be ready because we have been walking with Him. Only God knows the timing of Christ's coming. Our part is just to remain unspotted by the world and to walk in holiness and love.

SPIRIT, SOUL, AND BODY WHICH IS WHICH?

Dear Marilyn:
I get very confused when I hear pastors talk about our spirits, our souls, and our bodies. They say we are "a three-part being," and that "We **are** a spirit, we **have** a soul, and we **live in** a body." Is this all supported by the scripture?

Dear Friend:
This is supported by scripture, and we are certainly three-part beings. In 1 Thessalonians 5:23 we are told:

> "And the very God of peace sanctify you wholly; and I pray God your whole spirit and soul and body be preserved blameless unto the coming of our Lord Jesus Christ."

There it is: the spirit, the soul, and the body, which make up a whole person. Your spirit is your "new" or "regenerated" man. When you made Christ your Savior, your new spirit was given life by the Holy Spirit.

Your soul is made up of your mind, your emotions, and your will; it is the place where you make decisions. James 3:15 indicates that our souls must be submitted to our spirits: *"But this wisdom is not from above, but is earthly, sensual, devilish."* In this context the word *sensual* means "soulish." The wisdom of this world appeals to our mind and emotions, but it tends to "puff up," rather than "build up." But when—by our wills—we put God's Word first, then our spirits begin conforming our souls to the likeness of Jesus.

In 1 Corinthians 2:14 it speaks of soulishness: *"For the natural man receiveth not the things of the Spirit of God; for they are spiritually discerned."*

Who is the natural man? He is the one whose life is dictated by his mind and emotions. We can never understand the supernatural with our natural senses. That is why unsaved people don't understand spiritual things.

Some Christians even live soulishly, not discerning spiritual things. But you can have spiritual understanding, and Hebrews 4:12 tells you how: *"For the Word of God is quick and powerful, and sharper than any two-edged sword, piercing even to the dividing asunder of soul and spirit, and of the joints and marrow, and is a discerner of the thoughts and intents of the heart."* God's Word removes soulish thinking. For that reason Christians should never go one day without reading God's Word. If we want to be conformed to Jesus' image, we must take in His knowledge through our spirits.

A Christian whose soul is directed by God's Word is a spiritual Christian. He is not his own authority, but God is his authority. Live devoted to God's Word. Your spirit is the "candle of the Lord." He will illuminate all that you do!

IS LOUD PRAYING SCRIPTURAL?

Dear Marilyn:
Do you think that a person has to pray out loud in order to have his prayers answered? Someone who recently came to our church told us that unless we pray aloud, our prayers cannot be answered.

Dear Friend:
It is wonderful when we take advantage of every opportunity to pray aloud, but many times those opportunities simply aren't there. We often find ourselves in situations or circumstances where we cannot pray aloud. Let's not get so hung up on the **way** that we pray. Rather, let's recognize that at the end of our prayers are God's promises.

One of the greatest silent prayers is the prayer of Hannah in 1 Samuel 1. In her prayer for a son, Hannah moved her lips but made no audible sound. If you remember, she was misunderstood by the priest who was watching. He thought that Hannah was drunk, but his assumption did not offend her. She was a woman who knew how to stand fast and press through! Hannah shared her prayer request with the priest, and he then spoke his faith with hers. My, what a gift God gave Hannah! He gave her Samuel, who was followed by five more children!

Loud prayer, silent prayer, whatever the prayer—it must

be offered in faith in the name of Jesus, according to God's Word. Then it will be blessed and receive answers. My main suggestion to you is that you pray God's promises instead of problems.

God bless you in whatever manner you seek to pray.

Dear Marilyn,

Chapter Seven
PRAYER

- **Prayer Length**
- **Determining God's Voice**
- **Healing Prayers**
- **Long Distance Prayers**
- **Loud or Silent Prayer?**

PRAYER LENGTH

Dear Marilyn:
How long should I pray every day? I have friends who spend hours in prayer every day. I know this sounds terrible, but I get bored praying for even short amounts of time. Can I pray throughout the day, or does God want me to pray in one time slot? What does the Bible say?

Dear Friend:
First of all, stop comparing yourself with other Christians. Paul told his pupils, "Imitate me as I imitate Christ." In other words, Jesus—not other people—is your example. You need to behold Him instead of other Christians.

About prayer, Paul said, "Pray without ceasing." Does that mean we should quit our jobs, stay home, and pray all day? No, it doesn't mean that at all. Paul was indicating that God gave us the gift of praying in tongues so that we could be in communion with God all day. By praying in the Spirit, we can redeem what might otherwise be wasted time. I have found that praying in the Spirit is wonderful when I am driving my car, cooking dinner, and so on. If you think about it, God has given us many, many opportunities to pray throughout each day. Taking advantage of these opportunities, you can flow in a continuous refreshing of the Holy Spirit.

As far as setting aside daily prayer time, all Christians should pray every day. God's Word says that if we seek Him early, we will find Him. I like to take that scripture literally. In the morning your mind is like a blank slate—and that's the best time for God to write on it! Jesus said, "My sheep know My voice." But how will we know His voice if we don't take time each morning to hear it?

You don't have to pray for 10 hours every day. But give God some special time each day to prepare you for walking in His will. I want God's wisdom for my day, and I know that you do, too.

Perhaps you should start with 30 minutes of prayer each day. Remember to keep that time consistent. Then, if the Lord directs you to incease your prayer time, you can do that. Paul said, "Present our bodies as living sacrifices unto God." He called it our "reasonable service." If you think about it, Paul was right! After all, God knows what is best for us. He knows that prayer helps make His Word a reality in our lives.

DETERMINING GOD'S VOICE

Dear Marilyn:

I have difficulty knowing God's voice. Sometimes I have been sure that the Holy Spirit was leading me in one direction, and then everything crashed around me. There have been other times, however, when I knew that God was leading me. How can I know that the Spirit of God, and not my own thoughts and desires, is leading me?

Dear Friend:

John 10 offers you a wonderful promise that the Lord's sheep know His voice, and the voice of a stranger they will not follow. But I know the feelings you are having. There have been times when I felt certain that God was leading me, yet I discovered that the "leading" was nothing more than a fleshly thought. I have cried out in the same way that you are crying out: "God, show me how to walk by the Spirit."

God began to show me a helpful way to **know** that I am being led by the Spirit, and I want to share it with you. In Galatians 5:16 we are told, *"Walk in the Spirit and you will not fulfill the lusts of the flesh."* Basically, I have found that walking in the Spirit means that we are not walking by the instincts of our senses. To walk after the flesh means that we are living by what we smell, see, taste, feel, and hear. But to walk by the Spirit means to act on God's Word, no matter what sense-knowledge tells us. When Christians get "off base," they are usually walking according to senses, rather than by faith in God's Word.

Once I received several letters saying that I should go on the radio in a certain needy area of the United States. I asked my staff for counsel on this, and they said, "That situation would not produce enough positive results. Your efforts would be better spent in some other area or project." But I kept receiving letters from people who were saying, "We know that your program on this station would bring real benefits to all involved. You ought to go on radio here." Because of all the letters I was receiving, I made a personal decision to broadcast my program in that certain area.

I had prayed about the situation, but I hadn't **really** prayed for the leading of the Lord. Just as my staff had warned, the radio broadcast in this area never went anywhere. Eventually I had to admit that I went on that station from a personal leading, rather than a leading from the Holy Spirit. I had listened to the voice of my flesh and those around me, without seeking the voice of the Lord. Had I asked God for His leading, He could have directed me to use that money in a wiser way to benefit more people.

I believe that our flesh seeks after signs—something we can see or feel. But Jesus said, "A wicked generation seeks for signs." Such people are walking after their sense knowledge. We aren't supposed to look for signs. We are supposed to look for God's Word and allow signs to follow us!

Check out the leadings you have. Ask yourself, "Is this my flesh wanting a sign, or is this God's Word directing my spirit?" If you follow the Word, you will never be disappointed.

HEALING PRAYERS

Dear Marilyn:
Recently a young girl in our church died of leukemia, and her death has really caused me to have some doubts about healing. Every member of our church prayed and fasted, yet the girl still died. I've seen God's promises of healing in His Word, so this incident was very disappointing. We stood on the Word and believed God, but now I don't ever want to pray for the sick again. What am I supposed to think?

Dear Friend:
I am certain that every person who has prayed for the sick will understand your feelings. I had a similar situation in our church several years ago. At the time, I felt like saying, "God, what's the use in praying for the sick if they're going to die?" I felt so defeated. But one night when I was teaching a home Bible study, the Lord spoke to me from His Word in the book of Daniel. He used the example of the three Hebrew children who were to be thrown into the burning, fiery furnace.

The children spoke boldly to the heathen king, "Our God is able to deliver us." As I read that, my heart leaped, and the Holy Spirit said to me, "Your God is able to deliver you."

But when I read how the children said, "Even if God doesn't deliver us, we still won't bow to the heathen image."

Right then God sweetly spoke to my heart, "Marilyn, that is faithfulness. Will you be faithful even if it appears that your faith is failing?" His Words lifted my heart and I said, "God, I will be faithful even when I don't understand."

Jesus said, "When I return, will there be faith on the earth?" When I looked up the word **faith,** I found that it means "faithfulness." We may lose a few battles, but we still win the war. We must continue in faithfulness to obey God's Word, regardless of the circumstances. I am praying for you and your pastor.

LONG DISTANCE PRAYERS

Dear Marilyn:

One of my very dear loved ones lives in Korea and is in desperate need of healing. I feel that the Lord would have me lay hands on him, but I can't, because I cannot go to Korea. Somehow I don't feel sure that faith, without a point of contact, will bring healing. Do you have a scripture for this situation?

Dear Friend:

I have an excellent scripture for you, and then I want to share a personal experience that is just dynamite! Psalm 107:20 is your scripture, *"He sent his word and healed them, and delivered them from their destructions."* Just sending the Word of God to your loved one is your full assurance for his healing.

Once my mother's doctors found out that she had a brain tumor. When I heard the news, I was out of town, so I could not go lay hands on my mother. That night as I tried to sleep, a terrible, dark feeling of fear swept over me. That is when I first took hold of Psalm 107:20. The Holy Spirit brought it to my mind for the occasion—and I know that He gave me the same scripture for you.

I sent God's Word to the tumor in my mother's brain. In my mind, I could see the Word piercing the tumor and causing it to dissolve and disappear. I knew that God was healing my mother from the enemy's destructive intents. When she was X-rayed again by the doctor, there was no evidence that any tumor had ever existed. Today my mother walks in the perfect wisdom, love, health, and power of Jesus.

Since that time, I have seen Psalm 107:20 bring not just physical, but also mental and emotional healing to others. Isaiah said that God's Word would always prosper in the task to which you send it. Send God's Word to others daily. It will accomplish that for which you send it!

LOUD OR SILENT PRAYER?

Dear Marilyn:
I have a problem with people who pray loudly. I also have a problem with people who loudly praise the Lord. I feel that communicating with God doesn't have to be done at the top of one's lungs. Besides, I'm not the only one who is offended by those who are ridiculously loud. How do you feel about this?

Dear Friend:
I don't think that you are wrong. I think that God hears you when you are very quiet and even when you are silent. Some

of my greatest answers to prayer have been in uncomfortable situations when I had to pray silently about a very desperate need.

On the other hand, God isn't nervous. Some people enjoy expressing themselves loudly. They like to praise openly. I love what my husband tells our congregation every Sunday morning: "We don't care how you praise the Lord. If you want to be loud, be loud. If you want to dance, clap, or raise your hands, do it. But if you want to worship quietly and praise from your heart without outward expression, that's fine, too. We won't be unhappy with your silent worship, if you won't be unhappy with our loud worship."

I believe that God has simply called on His people to worship and pray, and that the volume in which we do these things is unimportant to Him. Let's not get hung up on whether a person is loud or quiet. The main thing is that we are praying and praising. When someone's prayer annoys you, leave that person with God. God richly bless you as you praise and pray. I deeply appreciate your hunger for both.

Dear Marilyn,

Chapter Eight
SIN

- **Sin Unto Death**
- **Regret Versus Repentance?**
- **Suicide**
- **Abortion**
- **Confrontation of Sinners**

"SIN UNTO DEATH"

Dear Marilyn:
The Bible talks about a "sin unto death" in the book of 1 John. Apparently, this sin is something that is committed by Christians rather than unbelievers. What is a sin unto death?

Dear Friend:
The reference for this scripture is found in 1 John 5:16b: *"There is a sin unto death: I do not say that he shall pray for it."* This scripture is talking about physical death, not spiritual death. We are told not to pray for a person who has committed a sin unto death.

Some people have shortened life spans because they continually choose to sin against God. That is a sin unto death. For example, King Saul's life was shortened because of his willful disobedience. God had anointed Saul, given him wisdom, and called him to be Israel's king. But Saul kept rebelling against God, and he also kept trying to kill God's chosen man, David. Eventually, Saul's disobedience led to his death, inflicted supposedly by an Amalekite who confessed his crime to David. Saul's life was shortened; however, David later wrote a psalm indicating that Saul was now in heaven.

Another sin unto death is found in the book of 1 Corinthians when Paul spoke of a man who had committed fornication with his father's wife. Paul said that the man's flesh should be committed to the devil so that his soul might be saved. I think that Paul was saying, "Let the devil have his flesh, let God have his soul, and let his life be shortened." But in 2 Corinthians you discover that the man repented, so God allowed his life to continue.

In the book of Acts, Ananias and Sapphira sinned unto death because they lied about their contribution to the church. God gave Ananias and Sapphira an opportunity to repent, but they refused to take it.

One more example is that of Hezekiah in 2 Kings 20. Isaiah told Hezekiah, "Set your house in order because you are going to die." But Hezekiah repented and prayed, so God gave him 15 more years to live. Hezekiah is the only person in the Bible who knew exactly what his span of life would be.

There is a sin unto death, as we find by searching the scriptures. But praise God, repentance can turn the "sin unto death" around and bring life!

REGRET VERSUS REPENTANCE?

Dear Marilyn:
My husband seems to have some deep problems in the way that he treats me and our children. He will do something to hurt us, then apologize, and seem very sorry. Then in a few months he will do the same thing again. His offense is nothing major, but it is just enough to keep our household in perpetual upset. I have seen this in other Christians. They claim to be sorry, but then they turn around and do the same thing again. Are they really sorry, and have they really repented?

Dear Friend:
Not knowing exactly what the problem is, I find your question a bit difficult to answer. However, let me share with you the difference between regret and repentance.

The Bible tells you that Judas, after betraying Jesus,

returned the 30 pieces of silver to the priest. Then Judas hung himself. If we repent, as 1 John 1:9 tells us, God is faithful and just to forgive our sins and cleanse us from all unrighteousness. Why wasn't Judas cleansed? Why wasn't his life transformed by his repentance? The Bible says that Judas *repented* (Matthew 27:3), so I looked up the word and found that it means "regretted."

Sometimes we just regret being caught. Sometimes we regret the consequences of our sin. But we are not deeply sorry for having offended God, so our hearts are not cleansed and transformed. True repentance involves godly sorrow. We are sorry that we have sinned against God. We recognize that sin is from the carnal nature and want to be cleansed from that carnality. Then when we confess our sins and receive cleansing from unrighteousness, transformation comes.

Hebrews 12 says that Esau sought a place of repentance but did not find it. He was sorry that he lost his birthright and the blessing, but Esau did not repent of his sinful nature. He had regret but not repentance, for the word *repent* means "to turn around and go in the other direction."

I understand where you are coming from. At times in my own life I have questioned, "God, if I was really sorry, then why did I sin again?" And the Lord showed me that I was simply in regret, not repentance.

David deeply repented of his sin with Bathsheba and the murder of her husband Uriah. His repentance brought a transformation. Never again did David become involved in an extramarital affair. He did a turnaround, didn't he?

Pray for your husband. Ask God to perform a work of deep repentance in his life by giving him godly sorrow. In 2 Corinthians 7:10 a, it says, "Godly sorrow works repentance to salvation." When we repent, we must ask God to take us beyond regret into repentance from offending Him and hurting others. When we do, cleansing takes place and we are set free to walk in the opposite direction of sin.

SUICIDE

Dear Marilyn:
Teen suicide is increasing, and it saddens me. But the impact of suicide never really hit me until a friend's brother killed himself. I know that my friend's family are Christians, but I'm not sure whether the brother who killed himself was a Christian. I'm so upset. Does the Bible say that every person who commits suicide will go to hell? If so, where does it say that?

Dear Friend:
The Bible gives the names of five men who committed suicide. One of them was Saul, Israel's first king, who intentionally fell upon his sword in battle. Another man who killed himself was Israel's king for just one week. The third suicide in the Bible was that of Samson who told God, "Let me die with the Philistines," when he caused the death of the primary Philistine leaders of that day. One of King David's counselors, Ahithophel, committed suicide by hanging himself. And, of course, Judas Iscariot also killed himself.

As you can see, these examples are quite varied. Saul was in a time of great disobedience to God when he killed himself, yet David wrote a psalm indicating that Saul was in heaven. Nor did Samson's suicide stop him from going to heaven, either. God used Samson's death to help him deliver Israel from Philistine oppression. The Bible says that Samson killed more in his death than he did in his life. Then in Hebrews 11, the "Hall of Fame of Faith," you see Samson listed as having been a faith hero.

Really the Bible never says that every person who commits suicide will go to hell or that God cannot forgive suicide victims. The only determining factor **today** to judge where people spend eternity is this: whether they accepted or rejected Jesus Christ as their Savior.

Many people who commit suicide lack sufficient knowledge on how to let Jesus help them overcome their problems. Perhaps nobody helped them reach that state of fellowship with the Lord. At any rate, the righteousness of Christ is a **gift** that we receive. No person goes to heaven because of the works they have achieved. If your friend's brother had the gift of Christ's righteousness, perhaps he just wasn't walking in the fellowship of that righteousness when he committed suicide. The Bible **never** says that all suicide victims go to hell, so I cannot make that statement.

ABORTION

Dear Marilyn:
As a Christian, I am very concerned to see the so-called Bible-believing Christians not taking a stand against abortion. I know that it's wrong to steal the lives of children called into existence by God. What can I say to someone who wants proof that abortion is wrong?

Dear Friend:
Scripture offers more than complete proof that unborn babies have completed personalities. At the moment of conception—perhaps even earlier—the tiny child's

personality begins forming. Psalm 139:14-18 tells us so:

"I will praise thee; for I am fearfully and wonderfully made. Marvelous are thy works, and that my soul knoweth right well.

My substance was not hidden from thee, when I was made in secret, and intricately wrought in the lowest parts of the earth.

Thine eyes did see my substance, yet being unformed; and in thy book all my members were written, which in continuance were fashioned, when as yet there was none of them.

How precious also are thy thoughts unto me, O God! How great is the sum of them!

If I could count them, they are more in number than the sand; when I awake, I am still with thee."

God sees our substance—all that we are and ever will be—while we are yet unborn! Exodus 13:2 tells you that when a firstborn child was conceived and had opened the mother's womb, the child immediately belonged to God: *"Sanctify unto me all the firstborn, whatsoever openeth the womb among the children of Israel, both of men and of beast: it is mine."*

Psalm 22:9,10 says, *"But thou art he who took me out of the womb; thou didst make me to hope upon my mother's breasts. I was cast upon thee from the womb; thou art my God from my mother's body."* The psalmist said, "Even before my birth, You were my God."

God creates and calls forth life. Who is man to determine whether an unborn child has the "right" to live or die? To abort a child is to deny it as being an individual separate from the mother. If a mother wants a child she calls it "a baby." But if the child is unwanted, she calls it "a fetus." But whatever you call it, that child was made by God: *"Did not he who made me in the womb make him? And did not one fashion us in the womb?"* (Job 31:15).

Isaiah 44:2a says, *"Thus saith the Lord that made thee, and formed thee from the womb."* Throughout the Bible God has emphasized the value of life in the mother's womb. He even revealed the personalities of certain people before they were born!

Jacob and Esau were both known by God before their births. God also told Jeremiah, *"Before I formed you in the belly I knew you. Before you came forth out of the womb I sanctified you and ordained you a prophet unto nations"* (Jeremiah 1:5).

God prenamed seven people in the Bible before their births, and several of them were named before conception! Deuteronomy 20:13 says, *"Thou shalt not kill,"* and the word *kill* means "murder." When abortion takes place, murder takes place. Every day in hospitals, doctor's offices, and clinics, the murders of babies are being committed. Many of those babies are so developed that if they were born in a hospital, they would live. It is my firm belief that the practice of abortion has brought a curse upon this country.

How can Christians stand against abortion? Proverbs 31:8 says, *"Open your mouth for the dumb in the cause of all such as are appointed to destruction."* There can be no such thing as a "neutral" or "uninvolved" stand in the life of a Christian. The unborn cannot open their mouths to cry out for justice against the stealing of lives. But we can cry out for them. Write to your senator and congressman and get as involved as possible with the measures it takes to rid our country of abortion. We dare not stand aside and do nothing. God says, "As much as you have done it unto the least of these, my brethren, you have done it unto me."

If you have had an abortion, I want to say that you can repent right now and be forgiven by God. When King David's baby died shortly after birth, David said, "He [the child] cannot come to me, but I can go to him." One day you will come face to face with your child. You can see that baby in heaven because your repentance brought forgiveness. Now what better step can you take than to stop someone else from committing the crime?

CONFRONTATION OF SINNERS

Dear Marilyn:

Isn't it scriptural for me to confront people about the sin in their lives? I would think that a Spirit-filled Christian would want to get his life straightened out. What do you think? I'm not judging. I really want to help.

Dear Friend:

It is easy for us to see another person's sin and not our own. Yet I will admit that some sins are very blatant, and God does want to deal with them. When the Lord showed me how to deal with sin in other people's lives, it came as a surprise!

I had been listening to bits and pieces of gossip about people, and I was repeating the information to my husband as "prayer requests." But one day God began to show me that these were not prayer requests, but tidbits of gossip I had no business sharing! Then He gave me a scripture on how to deal with other people's sins:

> *"And I sought for a man among them, that should make up the hedge, and stand in the gap before me for the land, that I should not destroy it: but I found none"* (Ezekiel 22:30).

God said, "You have become an expert gap-finder. But you are not being a gap-stander."

I asked, "How can I stand in the gap?" God showed me in Revelation 12:11 that Christians overcome the enemy in two ways: 1) by the blood of the Lamb and 2) by the word of their testimony.

God said, "The blood of the Lamb gives you authority to speak My Word over sin in people's lives." At that moment I told God, "Look no further. I will stand in the gap for other people." Now when I see sin in someone's life, I pray for him according to 1 John 1:9, *"When we confess our sins, He is faithful and just to forgive us and cleanse us from all iniquity."* I pray that the person will confess his sin and receive Jesus' cleansing from it.

I also pray over specific needs of that person. If a person is having financial strains, I pray according to Philippians 4:19, *"My God shall supply all your need according to His riches in glory by Christ Jesus."* For marital problems, I pray that Jesus' blood will "reconcile all things unto Himself."

God is not looking for gap-finders. He is seeking gap-*standers* who will pray His Word for people. Right now, tell God to look no further. Tell Him that you are willing to stand in the gap for your brothers and sisters. As you pray God's Word over them, His work will blossom in their lives.

Dear Marilyn,

Chapter Nine
THE MOVEMENT OF GOD

- How Can I Know God's Will?
- How Can I Cast Out Demons?
- Why Does Healing Take Time?
- How Do I Bless My Enemies?
- Do Words Work?

HOW CAN I KNOW GOD'S WILL?

Dear Marilyn:
I feel as though I can't find God's will for my life. Why is this so difficult? Must Christians struggle to know what God's will is for their lives?

Dear Friend:
I don't believe that God is playing hide-and-seek with Christians. He wants us to know His will collectively—as members of the Body of Christ—and individually, each with a personal calling. We don't have to struggle to know God's will for our lives.

I believe that knowing God's will is not as difficult as you have imagined it to be. Often we run around trying to do this, or do that, to be in God's will. But we don't realize that we are already in His will! I heard a man say, "If God is not checking or correcting your spirit, you must be in His will." That's simple, isn't it? I want to share three steps that will help you discern God's will for your life:

First, your desire should line up with the Word. Is your desire scriptural? God always leads us with His Word.

Second, you should have an inner witness of your leading. God confirms the Word with His Holy Spirit. The Holy Spirit bears witness with God's Word in your spirit. He will lead you into all the truth of the Word through an inner witness.

Third, circumstances should line up accordingly. At times, however, you may have a waiting period. Your desire may be scriptural, and you may have an inner witness, but circumstances may take some time before coming together. Be patient. If you are in God's will, circumstances will change. I want to assure you that it isn't God's will for you to stumble around trying to find Him. By faith, you CAN be sure and secure in Him.

HOW CAN I CAST OUT DEMONS?

Dear Marilyn:
How do you cast demons out of someone? How do you know that a person has a demon? Jesus told us that the sign of casting out devils would follow believers, but I'm afraid of it. My fear is based on the story told in the book of Acts about the seven sons of Sceva. I'm afraid that demons might try to attack me if I try to cast them out of another person. Please explain.

Dear Friend:
You have to be certain that you are spiritually prepared for this ministry. Be aware of the devil's devices so that you can discern evil spirits. It is true that Christians are in Christ; therefore, they have authority over demons. But we must be spiritually prepared for **any** ministry before God uses us in it.

Unbelief and fear will keep you from casting demons from a person. In the book of Matthew the disciples were unable to cast the devil from a young man with a spirit. They asked Jesus, "Why were we unable to cast out the devils?"

Jesus answered them, "Because of your **unbelief.**"

Here are some simple guidelines toward casting out a demon, and I'm sure they will be of some help.

1. Be certain that a person really wants to be delivered. If he doesn't, evil spirits will just come back. Any person who doesn't want help can have one thousand counseling appointments, but there will be no change until the desire to

change is present. The desire to change is the key to experiencing a change in mind and heart.

2. Be certain that the person knows and understands the authority in the name of Jesus. Also, be sure that the person understands that Jesus defeated Satan at Calvary. James 2:19 says, *"Thou believest that there is one God; thou doest well; the devils also believe, and tremble."* Why do devils tremble? Because they are defeated! A person must comprehend a Christian's God-given power and authority in Christ, and when you speak the Word of God, victory will come through!

3. You need to speak God's Word against the devil. No other word has power to defeat him. When Satan tempted Jesus in the wilderness, Jesus spoke God's Word, and He spoke it three times! Sometimes we get discouraged when dramatic results don't happen immediately. But don't be discouraged! The Word of God is always your most effective weapon.

4. Pray in the Spirit beforehand and be dependent on His divine guidance. In Matthew 12:28 you see that Jesus casts out evil spirits by the power of the Spirit of God. Build and strengthen your inner man by praying in the Spirit.

5. Use the name of Jesus! Command evil spirits to leave in Jesus' name, because they know the authority of that name. Mark 6:7 says that disciples were given power over unclean spirits. This power is yours as a disciple of the Lord Jesus Christ. Use it! Victory is certain when you know the authority of the One in whose name you speak.

I wanted to add, in reference to your question about the sons of Sceva, they were not casting out devils in the name of Jesus. They cast out devils "in the name of Jesus whom Paul preaches." Unless a person is born again by the Spirit of

God, they cannot speak the Lord's name with authority. It is understood that no person can cast out a demon without being a Christian—a born-again believer in Jesus Christ.

WHY DOES HEALING TAKE TIME?

Dear Marilyn:
Why are some people healed instantly, while others take a long time before being healed?

Dear Friend:
Often when believers lay their hands on sick people and pray for recovery, healing manifests instantly! It is a wonderful miracle. But when someone isn't instantly healed, it does not mean that they aren't receiving a miracle. When recovery is not immediate, it is important that we keep our faith intact in God's Word rather than in physical symptoms.

To be healed of sickness you must first believe God's Word. Then it can work in your life. God's Word is like a seed planted in your spirit. When you plant carrot seeds, you don't run outside the next day expecting to pick carrots! You plant the seed of God's Word in faith. You believe that Jesus took your infirmities and diseases, and by His stripes you were healed (1 Peter 2:24). You must water that seed every day by confessing God's Word, believing it, and trusting God for your healing. The day will come when healing is evident because the seed will have matured!

Years ago I suffered terribly from a severe back problem that was diagnosed as a malformed spine. This ailment was extremely painful, and my doctor said, "It can only get worse."

My husband laid hands on my back and prayed, and we believed together that God had healed me. But no outward healing was evident. In fact, my back grew visibly worse, and soon afterward I had to sleep on the floor to be comfortable at all. Then in the morning I could not stand up straight until almost noon. In spite of these symptoms, every day I confessed my faith in God's Word: "My back is recovering."

I believed and spoke God's Word relentlessly for almost six months. Then one morning I stood erectly and walked without a trace of pain! God healed my back that day, many years ago, and since then I have remained free from back problems.

I had to become stubborn about receiving that healing, but stubborness in God's Word pays off. God's Word says that "the violent" take His kingdom by force. You may have to be aggressive with your faith in order to have results. Then there are times when healing comes through an instant miracle. Either way, let's praise God that healing is available!

HOW DO I BLESS MY ENEMIES?

Dear Marilyn:
The Bible tells me to bless my enemies. Should I bless a person so that he can hear me? I would prefer to bless my enemies in prayer, but I want to be scriptural.

Dear Friend:
Sometimes I think that God allows us to have enemies just so that we have opportunities to bless them, pray for them, and do good to them! I have had such "opportunities."

Once a man in my city said some very ugly things about me

to his congregation. He even called me a "false prophetess." Personally, I wanted to tell the man off, but the Lord said, "How do I want you to treat your enemies?"

I answered, "Lord, You love them."

He said, "Treat them as I would treat them."

From that time on, whenever I heard the man's name spoken, I said, "Lord, bless him." Then one day God even gave me a special way to bless the man by promoting his church. I obeyed the Lord and saw the special fruits of obedience. Not long afterward, some people from the man's congregation called to say that their pastor's attitude had been transformed. He was not only speaking highly of me, he even invited his congregation to read through the Bible using my plan in TIME WITH HIM.

I asked God, "What happened?" He gave me the scripture, "When a man's ways please God, He makes even his enemies to be at peace with him." I don't think that you must speak God's blessings directly to a person. Sometimes an "enemy" may live so far away that this would be impossible. But bless enemies in your prayers, and pray that God will do good to them. Then—if possible—bless them with your actions. Send a caring letter just to make them feel special. If you will bless your enemies, pray for them, and do good to them, God will transform those relationships. When we choose God's way, we get miracles!

DO WORDS WORK?

Dear Marilyn:

Some of the faith teaching on confessing God's Word really turns me off. I see a lot of people confessing for

Cadillacs and new homes, but their lives are miles away from God's Word. Maybe I'm just skeptical, but do you really believe that words can change circumstances?

Dear Friend:

There is no question that God's power is first in our hearts and then in our mouths through our confession. Sometimes we see people confessing God's Word from their mouths, when it really isn't in their hearts. Often the very act of speaking causes miracles to happen. I've seen people's lives line up because of the words they were speaking. God's Word has a beautiful way of changing hearts. Remember, **hearing God's Word implants faith.**

Christians have a definite responsibility to be committed to the Word of God. Joshua 1:8 says, *"This book of the law shall not depart out of thy mouth."* Proverbs 18:21 says that death and life are in the power of the tongue, and we will eat the fruit of the words we speak. Our tongues will produce either positive or negative things. Matthew 12:36,37 confirms this: *"Every idle word that men shall speak, they shall give account thereof in the day of judgment. For by thy words thou shalt be justified, and by thy words thou shalt be condemned."* If our words either justify or condemn us, they must be very important. Without a doubt, our words determine our circumstances.

How can we make God's Word create a difference in our lives? Joshua 1:8 not only says that the Word shouldn't leave us, but it continues, *"Thou shalt meditate therein day and night, that thou mayest observe to do according to all that is written therein: for then thou shalt make thy way prosperous and then thou shalt have good success."*

When your heart is full of God's Word, you can speak it in

full assurance that He will create the fruit of your lips. Matthew 12:35 says, *"A good man, out of the good treasure of his heart, bringeth forth good things."* How?--by speaking the Word that is stored within!

The meditation and commitment to God's Word must accompany the speaking of it. Otherwise, we speak in idleness. But we should all be cautioned not to criticize those who are speaking the Word. We cannot judge the intents of other people's hearts. If the Word is not in someone's heart, the fruit will not be in his life. But if he is meditating and speaking it, then he can bring forth fruit—and so can you!

Dear Marilyn,

Chapter Ten
THE BODY OF THE CHURCH

- **Has the Charismatic Movement Crested?**
- **Can Women Be Deacons?**
- **Should the Church Help the Poor?**
- **Minister: How Can I Fight Criticism?**
- **What About Water Baptism?**
- **Can Divorcees Be Part of the Church?**

HAS THE CHARISMATIC MOVEMENT CRESTED?

Dear Marilyn:

Do you feel that the charismatic renewal, which was happening within various denominations, has crested? I am beginning to think that God is moving in another direction.

Dear Friend:

To claim that the charismatic renewal has crested is the same as saying that it was nothing more than a religious fad. It certainly is not a religious fad! God promised in Joel 2:28 that He would *"pour out of His Spirit upon all flesh"* and this prophecy was for the end time. Of course, all you need to do is read a newspaper and compare it with Bible prophecies to know that we live in the day when God will fulfill those prophecies.

Frankly, I do not believe that we have reached any kind of a "crest." I believe that we have experienced the early rain, but have yet to experience the early and the latter rain together. Pray with me that we will see the greatest outpouring that the earth has ever had. You don't even have to leave America to know how desperately this outpouring is needed! Remember, the scriptures about the outpouring of God's Spirit say that it will be upon **all** flesh.

CAN WOMEN BE DEACONS?

Dear Marilyn:

Do you think that God permits women to serve as deacons in the church? I understand that some Presbyterian churches allow women to serve as deacons. I go to a Pentecostal church, however, and they refuse to discuss the idea of a woman deacon. I can think of several women in our church who would make excellent deacons, but to our clergy it is unthinkable. How do you feel about this?

Dear Friend:
I believe very definitely that women can serve as deacons. As always, my reference for answering this and any question is the Word of God. Romans 16:1 refers to a woman named Phebe, *"a servant of the church which is at Cenchrea."* The Greek word for servant is *diakonon*. When I looked it up in the Greek, I found that this word is the same one that we use for *deacon*.

In Paul's first letter to Timothy, he said that deacons must have only one wife, plus he made several other stipulations (1 Timothy 3:11,12). I believe that deaconesses can be implied. I even believe that Paul's description of the requirement for a deacon's wife could be referring to women deacons.

What is a deacon? Basically it means "one who serves." In his church God has men **and** women who truly desire to serve and support the Body of Christ. God richly blesses all the women whom He has called.

Don't harass men if they refuse to allow women to hold offices as deacons. Just pray and allow God to take hold of those men's hearts. God will change their hearts, if necessary. Remember, promotion into any office—whether in our jobs or in church offices—comes from the Lord. We need not beat our way in, because when God opens doors, no man can close them.

SHOULD THE CHURCH HELP THE POOR?

Dear Marilyn:

I am very upset with my church because we have no program through which we can really help the poor. I know that Jesus told us to help the poor, so I am concerned about those areas where my church falls short. In fact, I am so deeply concerned about the matter that I am considering changing churches. Do you think that a church move would be the answer?

Dear Friend:

Please pray before you decide to attend another church. I think that too many people change churches almost as often as they change clothes. Then charismatics become "cruisamatics." Please, please, please stay in your church and pray to break the enemy's power. Faith works by love, so you must have a loving attitude toward your pastor and the congregation. Perhaps God placed you in the congregation so that you might be the one who is instrumental in producing a change.

Jesus said about the poor that we will have them with us always. Remember, we will never totally meet the needs of the poor. One of the things that has bothered me about some of the poor people who come to our church for help is that many of them don't want to work. God's Word says that a man who does not take care of his family is worse than an infidel (1 Timothy 5:8). If a person is unwilling to work, then perhaps his poverty will awaken him to the need of providing for himself. I think that programs that give, give, give, without helping people to work, can leave them with very poor self-images.

In our church we rarely give money to people unless we first know the background of the need. We do give food and clothing, but we still monitor that giving. Our church has been criticized for this, but we must be good stewards of God's money.

Perhaps your church does not have all the finances it needs to help the poor. I realize that in the Old Testament the synagogue helped care for the poor, but remember that the people paid triple tithes. Many of the members of our present-day churches pay no tithes, much less a triple tithe. It is not only your pastor's fault that your church does not have a program for giving, perhaps it is also the fault of the congregation. If we hold back our finances, how can the church do its job?

We need to be committed people in our giving. I have often found that those who criticize the church the most are the ones who never give. I recommend that you pray and ask God for divine wisdom and love in order to back your pastor and church. If a giving program is God's will for your church, He will open those doors as you hold fast in prayer.

MINISTER: HOW CAN I FIGHT CRITICISM?

Dear Marilyn:
Right now my church is going through a very difficult time, and things are getting worse every day. Some of the people who have been the strongest, most supportive members of the congregation have turned against me. They are contacting

others who are against me, and some of the people have even left the church. This is grievous to my heart. If I try to talk with the people, they won't listen. I don't feel at liberty to use the pulpit for disclosing my personal hurts. I am beginning to feel alternately helpless or—even worse—bitter. What should I do?

Dear Friend:

First of all, you must guard your own heart according to Proverbs 4:23, *"Keep thy heart with all diligence; for out of it are the issues of life."* This situation is going to be determined by the attitude in your heart.

Some time ago, I was deeply offended by a Christian. I felt that he was being very unjust toward me, and my first reaction was to say, "I'm going to call him and tell him off!"

But the Holy Spirit whispered to my heart, "How do you treat enemies?"

I answered, "I really don't want to think about that right now." But the Lord's voice was so strong in my spirit that I finally said, "I know, Lord. I'm supposed to pray for my enemies. I'm supposed to bless them and do good for them." I made a decision to act on the Word, to pray for the person who offended me, and do good for him if the opportunity and leading from the Holy Spirit arose.

God did lead me into a situation where I could help bring material benefit to that person, and I prayed for and blessed that person every day. Because of these things, God turned that enemy into a friend. In fact, he became extremely supportive of my radio and television ministry.

God says that when a man's ways please the Lord, He even makes the man's enemies to be at peace with him. If you will make the decision to go God's way, you will enjoy God's results. But if you sow bitterness, you will reap bitter results. May God richly bless you, and I am praying for you.

WHAT ABOUT WATER BAPTISM?

Dear Marilyn:
I'm tired of doctrinal differences, dialogues and dogma on baptism. One person sprinkles, another immerses. Some baptize infants, others baptize when a person becomes a Christian. There are even those who insist that without baptism a soul cannot be saved. Who is right?

Dear Friend:
This is an excellent question. For the answer you must look to God's Word, which the THE truth. First of all, I believe that infant baptism has been incorporated in the church as a sincere act of dedication. However, the Bible says that repentance must accompany baptism. A baby has not sinned, nor can he repent, so he doesn't need to be baptized. Dedication of a child by his parents can be done, but nobody can make another person's decision to be saved.

I do believe that water baptism should follow a person's decision for Jesus. Baptism is a wonderful statement to the world that testifies, "I'm a new creature in Christ. Now I am being baptized in obedience to God's Word." Jesus was baptized, His disciples were baptized, and as new disciples, we should also be baptized. Often water baptism is a new Christian's first act of obedience to the Father!

Regarding the question of whether to sprinkle or immerse, you will find your answer has been lost in translation. The word *baptize* was transliterated—rather than translated—from the word *baptizo,* meaning "to immerse." Jesus was immersed in water at His baptism; Matthew 3:16 speaks of the Lord coming "up out of" the water.

Does water baptism save the soul? The thief on the cross next to Jesus was not water baptized. Yet Jesus told the thief, *"Today you will be with me in Paradise."* The man's soul was saved without water baptism. Take assurance in the Lord's own words that water baptism in itself does not save a person's soul.

Jesus said that we must be born again to enter the kingdom of God. The Bible never says that baptism is necessary for us to obtain salvation. However, if you haven't been water baptized yet and you are a born-again Christian, I would recommend it! Why? Because baptism is a command from God's Word, and it is a **blessing** for you. Act in obedience. You'll be blessed!

CAN DIVORCEES BE PART OF THE CHURCH?

Dear Marilyn:

I am a divorcee, and I do not feel accepted in my church. We live in a small town, and I attend the only charismatic church, so I cannot change churches. My two children (ages four and seven) and I need some caring Christian fellowship. Nothing at our church is geared toward the unique responsibilies and hardships faced by single parents. I feel so lonely, but I don't know what to do.

Dear Friend:

First of all, instead of seeking others who can minister to you, start seeking opportunities for ministering to others.

Ask your pastor how you can bless the church. Make yourself and your children available to bless others. No matter what your pastor suggests, carry it out joyfully as unto the Lord. Remember, your labor in the Lord is never in vain!

At home, speak positive, happy things about the services to your children. Reinforce in them a positive attitude about the Lord and His people. As your words and labors minister to others, the law of sowing and reaping will be enacted in your life. When you sow ministry, God brings ministry to you.

Perhaps you are the one whom God has chosen to initiate a program for single parents. How many single parents would come into the Kingdom because of such a program? This world is **full** of single parents needing what you can offer. I know that God will do tremendous things by causing your life experience to help others as you bring the Word into it. I am sure that the Holy Spirit has refreshed and helped you many times. Those are things that you could share with others.

Look for opportunities and open doors. I believe that the worst is over, and the best is just beginning.

Dear Marilyn,

Chapter Eleven
PASTORS AND MINISTRIES

- Discontentment With Pastor and Congregation
- Pastor Outside the Scriptures
- Evil Gossip About Ministries
- Wearing Other Ministers' Mantles
- Choice of Leaders in the Ministry
- Lazy Assistant Pastor

DISCONTENTMENT WITH PASTOR AND CONGREGATION

Dear Marilyn:
My pastor has let me down during a major crisis in my life. When I could not get him to help me, I called my Christian friends, who "couldn't be bothered" with me. Christians—the ones that I thought I could count on—have let me down. Why go to church or see another Christian again? These people don't even know how to be friends in times of need. I feel bitter and I cannot control it.

Dear Friend:
Bitterness is a luxury that you cannot afford, and it is something that spreads like cancer. It is so expensive that it will cost you your emotional, mental, physical, and spiritual health. First, keep in mind that as a Christian you cannot afford the luxury of bitterness.

Proverbs 25:19 says, *"Confidence in an unfaithful man in the time of trouble is like a broken tooth and a foot out of joint."* Every person reading this could say, "I have been disappointed by Christians." I am curious whether you have ever let someone down. I am sure that both you and I have. We don't do it intentionally. Perhaps we were either unthoughtful or even selfish, but we do not hurt others purposely.

In a sense, all of us have been a "broken tooth" or a "foot out of joint" to another person. Because of this, we cannot be bitter toward those who have done the same. We must do one of two things: 1) either forgive the person who offended us or 2) plan on never sinning again. God says that He will forgive us as much as we forgive others.

The bottom line is found in where we have placed our confidence. It isn't wise to put our confidence in human flesh. We can only be confident in the Lord.

Deal with your disappointment right now. Repent of having nurtured bitterness in your heart, and leave those people with God. Just because they let you down doesn't mean that God let you down. Flesh cannot bring you through a trial; only God's Word will bring you through. Flesh will wither and fade like the grass, but God's Word will endure forever.

Consider Jesus. He did not faint or grow weary, even though He bore our sinners' plight. The Bible reminds us that we have not resisted temptation unto the shedding of blood. Yet Jesus, in resisting sin, sweat great drops of blood at Gethsemane.

Look to God and say, "You will bring me through." Remember, the game is not over. You are to play until you win. God wants you to triumph in Christ, and you will—if your confidence is in Him.

PASTOR OUTSIDE THE SCRIPTURES

Dear Marilyn:
I am furious with my pastor because he hasn't handled some sensitive issues in a scriptural manner. I want to tell him off, but every time I'm prepared to do so, I think of the scripture where God says, "Don't touch My anointed ones." What should I say to my pastors? I'm afraid that if I say anything, this anger and resentment is going to spill out.

Dear Friend:
You are experiencing the harsh result of strife, and unless

you want to reap serious results, you must deal with it immediately. Galatians 5:15 says that strife will literally chew on you until it eats you alive! What is strife? It is hostile opposition that occurs as a result of differing viewpoints.

First of all, you need to get before God and **pray.** Ask God to give you a love in your heart for your pastor. Then set up an appointment to talk with him, rather than catching him off guard. Make your number-one goal of this appointment that of reconciling the situation to bring peace. You **will** bring peace, since you are acting according to the Word of God: *"If thy brother shall trespass against thee, go and tell him his fault between thee and him alone: if he shall hear thee, thou hast gained thy brother"* (Matthew 18:15).

The scripture says that if you approach a person in the above manner and that person doesn't receive you, then you can bring a neutral party into conference. If your point is still unreceived, then act scripturally by continuing in prayer until the matter is resolved.

God will give you marvelous opportunities to shed His love abroad in your heart toward your pastor or anyone with whom you disagree. Look for miracles and let God bring the supernatural into your relationships with others. Your pastor needs your love, and you need to be an overcomer.

EVIL GOSSIP ABOUT MINISTRIES

Dear Marilyn:
Lately I've heard some terrible things against people in well-known and popular ministries. Even the newspapers have carried some of these stories! Could there be any truth to them, or is this just the devil's attack against leadership in the Body of Christ?

Dear Friend:
I cannot give you a perfect answer because I could not possibly know the heart of every ministry, nor that of every minister. But the important thing is that all of us, individually, allow God to search our hearts daily so that we might have clean hearts before Him. Sometimes people in full-time ministry become too involved with ministering and lose involvement with the One to Whom they are ministering.

Recently the Lord really dealt with me as I was praying about "my ministry." As I prayed, it seemed that the Holy Spirit spoke strongly and sweetly to my spirit. "Marilyn, I am not as concerned about your ministry as I am concerned about your relationship with Me. Your ministry is simply an extension of our relationship together."

Sometimes in ministry, ministers tend to put their ministries first and their relationships to God second. When that happens, God has to remind them to put Him first. Then the rest of what flows forth is the manifestation of that relationship.

When you hear negative things about ministries, carry them to your heavenly Father in prayer, instead of to other Christians. If a ministry is wrong, God can correct the situation. Keep in mind that God did not call us to correct one another, but to pray for one another. Let God handle any wrong situations, because He knows how to do it.

WEARING OTHER MINISTERS' MANTLES

Dear Marilyn:
When I hear certain people speak who are active in the full-time ministry, I long to have their ministries. At first I used to think that these desires were just carnal. Now, however, I am

beginning to believe that my desires are spiritual. I especially think so after reading about how Elisha desired the mantle of Elijah's ministry—and in double portion! Can I take hold of the "mantle" of other people's ministries?

Dear Friend:
Your attraction to other people's ministries is not uncommon. Very often we are attracted to the strong anointing and powerful results that surface in certain ministries. We should respect and pray for those ministers, but to take hold of their "mantle" or ministry must be a direct leading and calling of God in our lives.

When reading the account of Elijah and Elisha in the book of 1 Kings, I see that even before the two met, Elijah knew that Elisha would receive the mantle (1 Kings 19:19). Sometimes we want to run after a ministry, rather than to run after the true Minister—the Lord Jesus Christ. When we seek Him, He will confirm our callings.

Ministries must be strongly confirmed in our spirits, in God's Word, and in the witness of reliable believers. God has a unique ministry for you in His field of harvest, as He has for every believer: *"For we are his workmanship, created in Christ Jesus unto good works, which God hath before ordained that we should walk in them"* (Ephesians 2:10).

God has set aside a work that only you can achieve. He has a mantle that is yours alone: the mantle of serving Him.

Once I complained to the Lord, "My schedule is just too wild! My life and ministry aren't nomal."

He answered, "You are comparing your life with the lives of other people. You're trying to wear someone else's mantle. Marilyn, you do live a normal life. This is normal **for you.**"

Find God's "normal" for your life. Take on the mantle of serving Him according to His Word. Everything else that blossoms forth is an extension of your relationship with Him. You will soon discover yourself walking in the good works that God has ordained for you. That's the mantle that will fit you perfectly.

CHOICE OF LEADERS IN THE MINISTRY

Dear Marilyn:
I have a small ministry with 20 employees. There have been a few times when I have placed the wrong people in positions of leadership, and the results were disastrous. I feel so disappointed when this happens. Not only does it bring strife and confusion to my staff, but outsiders also become wounded. I prayed before hiring those staff members. What went wrong?

Dear Friend:
Every full-time minister probably knows the frustrations of hiring someone who is wrong for a job. It can be absolutely devastating! Once after I made such a mistake, the Lord gave me a valuable lesson on hiring employees. He said, "You have been hiring people according to their ability, rather than their character." Then the Lord showed me Paul's letters to Timothy. Paul instructed Timothy, "Find faithful men and put them to work."

God said to me, "Look for faithfulness first. It's character; it's the fruit of the Spirit. Then look for ability." Ability can be developed, but character comes less easily. When you are hiring staff members, pray that God will send you men and women who are faithful. Then ask God for help in developing those people's abilities. Perhaps God would even have you train those people personally. But whatever the case, remember that character is the first, most important trait.

A final key for hiring good staff members is to spend time praying in the Spirit. In 1 Corinthians 2:15 it says, *"He that is spiritual judgeth all things."* Another translation says, *"He that is in the Spirit makes spiritual judgments."* God bless you. The Holy Spirit will lead you into all the truth. He will show you who the best workers are.

LAZY ASSISTANT PASTOR

Dear Marilyn:

I am a pastor who is stuck with a lazy assistant pastor. He has been with me for two-and-a-half years, and nobody else seems to notice his laziness. I am fed up with the man's slothful attitude, but the people in the church love him dearly. He is very popular, so I could make many people angry by terminating his employment. You're a pastor's wife—how would you handle this?

Dear Friend:

My very first suggestion is that you pray for God's wisdom in your communication with your assistant pastor. This may take some time, but it is important that you definitely hear from God. God doesn't play "hide-and-seek" with us. He wants to give you the wisdom you need.

Once I had a staff member with a great deal of responsibility, and he was always murmuring about his job. His short temper flared several times in confrontations with my staff, and also with me. Of course, my first instinct was to tell him off, but I didn't want to create problems. Mishandling a situation without God's wisdom is never the way to obtain solutions.

After setting aside a special time of prayer about this man's conduct and waiting for God's wisdom, I received a scripture: *"Godliness with contentment is great gain"* (1 Timothy 6:6).

I confronted the man and said, "I love you, but I know that you are unhappy about the pressure in your job. I have been praying for you." Then I told the man about the scripture that God gave me for him. I said, "You have not been a gain to yourself, to your work, or to God's kingdom." Then I asked, "Can you pinpoint the area where you are discontented? Is it with God? With me or your job? Are you discontent with yourself? Because until you are content, you cannot be a gain to anyone."

That Spirit-inspired message flowed into the man's heart and caused tears to well up in his eyes. He began to weep as he told me, "I am discontent with myself." At that moment the Lord set the man free, and he became an asset to our staff.

God has the perfect answer for your situation with your assistant pastor. First, pray for God's wisdom. Let God give you the answer—don't suggest the answer to God. Second, give the man a daily schedule of what you expect to be accomplished. Request the schedule back at the week's end. Commend the man's achievements and correct the unfinished tasks. Finally, if the man does not come through, ask God to cause the situation to be one where he leaves peacefully. God loves you and your church, so be assured that He will also give you wisdom.

Dear Marilyn,

Chapter Twelve
UNCHRISTIAN CHRISTIANS

- **Carnal Christians**
- **Up-and-Down Christians**
- **The Backslider and Salvation**
- **Materialistic Christians**
- **Unchristian Christians**
- **Prophecy or Misdirection?**

CARNAL CHRISTIANS

Dear Marilyn:
Some of the Christians in my church are really carnal. They don't commit themselves to church attendance, I'm sure they don't read their Bibles daily, and if you call a prayer meeting, forget it. Many of these so-called Christians attend worldly functions that, I think, would displease God. If God wants us to be holy, why do so many Christians have a problem making a commitment?

Dear Friend:
There is no question that God is holy. His Word is holy, His Spirit is holy, and His Son is holy. As a result, God's people are also to be holy.

When we are born again, we receive in our spirits the incorruptible seed of God's Word. Once a person told me that any seed, cut in half and placed under a microscope, will display exactly what it will become. In every seed is a picture of the finished product! I believe it is the same with the seed of God's Word in His people.

When we were born again, we received the seed with the picture of Jesus Christ. Every Christian has the potential to become as the image of Christ to others. But whether we fulfill that image is a personal decision. Every day Christians must decide which image they will fulfill: the image of the old man or that of the new.

Your concern for the Body of Christ is good, but make sure it isn't judgmental. Try to look at each Christian as having the potential of Jesus inside. Sometimes it's too easy for us to compare ourselves with other Christians. But 2 Corinthians 10:12 tells us that it isn't wise for Christians to compare themselves one to another—and if it isn't spiritual, it must be carnal. Sometimes I think that we grade ourselves "on a curve" by looking at others. But God doesn't grade us on a curve. He grades us on His Word. Don't compare yourself with other Christians, but only to the Word of God. When you look at Christians, look for the image of Jesus inside, and see their potential. Your faith for that potential can bring it to pass in someone's life.

God is going to help you love the people in your church as Jesus would love them. I appreciate your question.

UP-AND-DOWN CHRISTIAN

Dear Marilyn:
I feel like a yo-yo Christian. One day I'm up and the next day I'm down. One day I can face anything, and the next day every circumstance overwhelms me! I know that God doesn't want me wavering. I know that faith is supposed to change this, but somehow it hasn't sunk in. I want to be a strong Christian, but I don't know how to be one.

Dear Friend:
Every day we, as Christians, have opportunities for either defeat or victory. Those who are victorious are the ones who won't accept defeat. They turn down defeat by taking hold of God's Word and letting it pull them through the temptation to quit.

Luke 18:27 says, *"The things which are impossible with men are possible with God."* By staggering from your circumstances, you are observing them from a human point of view. But circumstances change when we see them from God's angle! Suddenly the impossible becomes possible.

I looked up the word *possible* in Luke 18:27, and it means "miracle-working power." Jeremiah 32:27 says, *"Behold, I am the Lord, the God of all flesh; is there anything too hard for me?"* We must consider our circumstances and then realize that—with God—we have miracle-working power to change them. You have been trying to resolve difficult circumstances through your own ability. But the weakness of human flesh cannot change circumstances. When you are weak, God wants to come on the scene and be strong in you!

God told Abraham that Sarah would have a baby. At age 89, Sarah thought, "Me? Impossible!" When she laughed at the thought, God heard her and confronted her about it. But then God had the last laugh—He named the baby **Isaac**, which means "laughter."

I always say, "God will get the last laugh if we allow Him to have it." Hebrews 11, the Bible's "Hall of Fame of Faith," tells you that Sarah, with all her human frailty, had **faith** for a baby. With faith in God's ability, any situation becomes possible. There is no need for you to be unstable when your life is in God's hands.

Jesus' disciples asked Him, "Can God really save rich, hardened, rebellious people?" Jesus answered His disciples, "With men, it is impossible, but not with God." Jesus was saying, "Even impossible circumstances aren't too big for God to handle."

A man's demon-possessed son was freed when Jesus told the father, "If you can believe, all things are possible." You get your strength and stability from God's Word. You need to bring God's promises continually into your day. Every step of the way, look at your life through God's Word, instead of through your senses. Sense knowledge is fickle. If you are living by sense knowledge, you will continue to be up and down. But every time you turn an opportunity for defeat into victory, you grow stronger in the Lord's strength.

Jesus faced the tempter, the devil, as a man. But Jesus won by saying, "It is written." When you face temptation, with God's Word you'll win, too!

THE BACKSLIDER AND SALVATION

Dear Marilyn:
Why is it so difficult for people to act born again after they are saved? I have a friend who backslides as soon as he makes a new commitment to God. Do Christians actually backslide, or do they lose their salvation?

Dear Friends:
When an unbeliever receives Jesus Christ as Savior, that person is literally **born again** in his spirit. He has the seed of a brand new nature! However, new Christians have not yet had their minds renewed to God's Word. We all have to deal with our old natures, which have been trained according to the flesh. Backsliding is what happens when a Christian relies on his old nature, rather than his new nature. As a result, sin produces sin in that person's life.

I compare the new and old natures like this: the old nature is a "pig" nature and the new nature that God imparts to us is a "lamb" nature. The saddest thing about a backslidden Christian is that he is miserable. He has known the ways of righteousness and cannot enjoy living in a "pigpen."

With this in mind, it is reassuring to know that God does love the backslider. The Lord is ever watching and desires to draw backslidden people back by the power of the Holy

Spirit. For example, look at the parable of the prodigal son. The young man's father never stopped watching for his son to come home. When he returned, the son was given the very best that his father had.

It's not fun to live in a pigpen, and it's not fun to smell as though you've been in one. But I don't believe that backsliders living in the world's pigpen are actually lost. I believe that they are out of fellowship with God. They are miserable.

If you desire to counsel your friend about his backsliding, tell him that God has a first-aid kit for backsliders. It is called **repentance**. I always say, "Don't run from God. Run to Him." Remember, when a Christian receives Jesus as Savior, then Jesus asks to be that person's **Lord** and **Master**. When we confess our sins, the Lord is faithful and just to forgive us and cleanse us from all unrighteousness (1 John 1:9). Then He can be the Lord of our lives!

MATERIALISTIC CHRISTIANS

Dear Marilyn:

This prosperity teaching, which I have been hearing, upsets me a great deal. I am finding that Christians are focusing on material things rather than spiritual matters. To put it bluntly, they are seeking God's hands, not his face. How do you feel about this overemphasis on prosperity?

Dear Friend:

I don't think that any Christian should make material prosperity the ultimate goal. Rather, we seek prosperity of our souls by putting God's Word first in our lives. There is no question that God wants us to be financially prosperous, but first we are supposed to prosper in the things of God. The Bible says, *"Beloved, I wish above all things that you might prosper and be in health, even as your soul prospers"* (3 John 2).

If we have prosperous souls, we won't have to be after money—money will be after us! Proverbs 3:13,14 confirms, *"Happy is the man that findeth wisdom, and the man that getteth understanding. For the merchandise of it is better than the merchandise of silver, and the gain thereof than fine gold."* Again, here is prosperity of soul. We need the wisdom of God's Word in our souls before we receive the riches, long life, and honor.

When Solomon prayed for wisdom, God was so pleased with this request that He said, "Since you asked for wisdom, I'm also going to give you riches, honor, length of days, and peace." Solomon wanted soul prosperity, but every area of his life was prospered by God!

God does want Christians to be prosperous, but He wants to be the One who prospers us. Remember that as we seek first the kingdom of God, the other things will be added to us. And that's God's promise!

UNCHRISTIAN CHRISTIANS

Dear Marilyn:
When I was first born again and baptized in the Holy Spirit, it seemed like every day was full of joy and the power of the Holy Spirit. I loved going to church. I loved reading my Bible. And I loved being with other Christians. But now it seems that my Christian experience is growing sour. I've seen many hypocrites in church. I've been let down by Christians and have found out that many Christian leaders are not as

spiritual as they should be. What is wrong with me? What is wrong with the Body of Christ?

Dear Friend:

At some time or other, every Christian faces these kind of struggles. Jesus is the same yesterday, today, and forever. He said that He would never leave you or forsake you. So He hasn't moved. If you are not enjoying your Christian life as you once did, Christ hasn't moved—but perhaps you have. What were you doing in the early part of your Christian life that you are not doing now? Or maybe I should ask, what are you doing now that you weren't doing then?

We always have to be "moving on" with God. It's like going up a steep mountain and having no brakes. You are either moving with God or you are rolling backwards.

Perhaps you have been spending time gossiping about other Christians. There is nothing worse than gossiping to rob you of your joy. When we begin to open our ears to garbage, we find that garbage begins to have an effect on us. Repent, confess your sins, and begin to do the things that you once did when you first began your relationship with Christ.

Nothing is worth doing if we lose the presence of God. There is a spiritual thermometer built into the center of your being. The Holy Spirit is warning you that something is wrong. But the good news is that you can do something about it! Get into your Bible. Get on your knees. Repent of any area where you have been foolish or in sin. And let Jesus take the struggles out of your life. He loves you and I do, too.

PROPHECY OR MISDIRECTION?

Dear Marilyn:

I recently visited someone who told me, "I have a word from the Lord for you." She then told me that I was to stop buying so many new clothes and give her a part of the money I was spending. I do have quite a large wardrobe, so her words were somewhat convicting. Could God have been correcting me for buying too many clothes? Should I give some of them to this person? I feel somewhat convicted. But I'm still not positive that this was a word from God.

Dear Friend:

I am strongly opposed to people who invite Christians into their homes for "coffee, tea, and prophecy." A word from the Lord should only confirm the Word that is already in your heart. It disturbs me to see sincere Christians being misdirected by people who abuse God's Word.

If someone gives you a "word from the Lord," ask the person if he is willing to present the message to your pastor. Your pastor has been placed by God over the congregation to care for them. Pastors are to be spiritual guides who can check out situations like yours. Many times people with "a word" for you are against those who hold positions of leadership. That in itself is dangerous! God placed a divine order in the body of Christ for our safety.

Go to your pastor about such situations; insincere people want to avoid any confrontations from those in authority. In fact, many people who are giving out "words from the Lord" have never even read through the Bible! Their lives aren't clean, nor are their motives. They are merely exalting themselves to gain popularity or control. Paul warned about such people. He called them "ravenous wolves among the flock." Why does a wolf come? He comes to tear and divide God's people.

You have a Bible, which God has called, "a more sure word of prophecy." Use God's Word to discern right from wrong. Ask the Holy Spirit to lead you into all truth. I am praying that you will walk in His wisdom.

Dear Marilyn,

Chapter Thirteen
MISCELLANEOUS THINGS

- **Food for the Communists**
- **Wasted Time**
- **Dealing with Correspondence**
- **Loser or Winner**
- **Make-up for Christians**

FOOD FOR THE COMMUNISTS

Dear Marilyn:

I am so upset by the horrible famines that are happening in communist countries, particularly in Ethiopia. The communist leaders oppress their people and don't care about the fact that they are dying from starvation. My question is, "Should we even be feeding people who live in communist countries?" How can it be right to feed and help such ungodly people?

Dear Friend:

There is no question that the communist government is at enmity with us. God has told us how to treat the communist people in Matthew 5:44, *"Love your enemies, bless them that curse you, do good to them that hate you, and pray for them."*

I certainly am not condoning the doctrine of communism. I have seen its hideous, demonic, devilish effects on too many people's tragic lives. But we Christians cannot sit back and allow people to starve when it is in our power to help. In fact, I believe that one reason for America being so blessed today is because she is a country that feeds many of the world's hungry people. Let's take advantage of our opportunities to bless those people by bringing them not only food, but also, whenever possible, the gospel.

WASTED TIME

Dear Marilyn:

I know that you have a busy schedule, so you can probably answer this question: How can I stop being a procrastinator?

Dear Marilyn

I never seem to accomplish what is necessary in one day. I know that I habitually waste time, but I've always been this way. There must be some way that I can make my schedule work in my favor, not against me.

Dear Friend:

Time is very precious. I would call time one of our most valuable resources! Time cannot be stored and saved, and all of us possess 24 hours in each day. It would be good if all Christians must be aware of their need to be good stewards over the time God gives them. Time is *a* gift from God, and we must not waste it. Realizing this fact is "step one" toward making a change.

Psalm 90:12 says, *"So teach us to number our days that we may apply our hearts unto wisdom."* In this context, the word **number** means "to organize." The psalmist was saying, "Teach us to organize our activities so that our days will be filled with wisdom." God wants to reveal how you can organize your day. But He cannot reveal His wisdom to you unless you put Him first in each day's beginning. Seek the Lord early, in prayer, and in the Word, and He will show you how to set up your daily activities.

Ephesians 5:16 tells you to *"redeem the time, for the days are evil."* The word **redeem** means "to buy back or recover." God wants to help organize your time first. Then He wants to help you buy back the best opportunities from your day so that you can achieve more than other people! God wants to give you an advantage with your time.

The book of Proverbs tells you that the Lord also will "lengthen" our days. He will cause you to achieve twice as much as other people in one day! These benefits from God's Word are just for Christians. It is exciting to know that God

Miscellaneous Things

has these promises for how we spend our time.

Let me give you four hints for overcoming procrastination and getting the most from your schedule:

- *First of all,* begin each day with prayer and time in studying God's Word. Jesus never lost sight of His goals, because they were centered on God's Word. With the Word and fellowship with God as your first priority, you will bring the supernatural into your activities.
- *Second,* make a daily list of what you need to achieve. This makes your goals tangible and easier to accomplish. It helps you organize the best plan for getting things done in the right order.
- *Third,* develop a weekly activity schedule. Long-range planning is as vital as short-range planning! Assign all of your activities to the day in which it is to be accomplished.
- *Fourth,* remember to schedule time for problems or interruptions. That way, if something unexpected comes up, your schedule is still preserved.

Follow through with these four rules for successful organization of time. Don't let your emotions dictate your activities. We may not always feel like finishing certain things. But when we discipline ourselves to go beyond our feelings, we obtain the success of God's promises!

Keep your eyes on specific goals and be committed to accomplishing them. Jesus had timetables and God has timetables. Both of Them set goals, and the Holy Spirit wants to help us reach our goals. Let the Holy Spirit redeem your time and make every day the best day of your life!

DEALING WITH CORRESPONDENCE

Dear Marilyn:

This may seem silly, but I know that you must have an answer, since you deal with so many people. I think that God is going to use me to minister in mighty ways, and I am trying to concentrate on spending my time with Him in preparation for ministry. The problem is: I find myself doing small amounts of correspondence that take up a great deal of my valuable time! I do not type, so all my letters are written in longhand before my secretary gets them. It takes me forever to wade through my daily correspondence. How did you handle this time-bandit in your early stages of ministry?

Dear Friend:

I know what it is to deal with the painstaking process of correspondence! I don't type, and, as a joke one year, my staff presented me with a certificate that said, "This is the Ministry Gift of Typewriting." Even that didn't work!

In the early stages of ministry it was next to impossible to write my articles, plus squeeze out enough time to stay on top of correspondence. I thank God that He was faithful to help me in those things. But I found my answer to the problem while I was ministering one day in Chicago.

As a young woman watched me write longhand in a notebook, she asked, "What are you doing?" I told her, "I am writing the daily devotions for my magazine."

When the woman discovered that I did not type, she met me after the next meeting and presented me with a beautifully-wrapped, small package containing a tiny, purse-sized tape recorder. From then on, I recorded my letters and articles on the machine. An additional, inexpensive attachment made it possible for my secretary to transcribe and edit those letters. That "secret" solved the problem of endless writing, and I use that same method today! In no time I can have letters ready to be typed, and it is efficient for everyone involved. I encourage you to enjoy the great economy of time that is awaiting you!

LOSER OR WINNER

Dear Marilyn:

No matter what I do, whether on the job or at home, I always feel like a failure. All my life I've been told that I couldn't measure up or that I would never amount to anything. I can't really think of myself as anything more than a loser. I already know that I have a bad self-image. But what I really need to know is whether there is hope for me to change the way I think. I don't know what to do.

Dear Friend:

You are contradicting what the Word of God says about you. God says that you are a winner. But you are blocking out the truth by saying, "No, I'm not. I'm a loser." You are reinforcing the lies that the devil has told you. You must take great hope in what God has promised for you!

God has given you a very important message that you are supposed to be a winner. He didn't say that you will only win once in a while. He didn't say that you will only win sometimes. God's Word says that you **always** triumph in Christ. God says that you are **more than** a conqueror through Christ who loves you. Philippians 4:13 says that you can do **all** things through Christ who strengthens you. Jesus will give you the strength and ability to overcome a poor self-image.

When God sees you, He isn't concerned with your outward appearance or how much education you have had. God never measures your IQ. He measures your "I can's." You CAN do all things through Christ. If your own ability makes you feel like a failure, that's all right. You have Christ's ability, and His ability within you is perfect.

Genesis 1:26 tells you that God made you in His own image. Through that image you were given dominion over the devil. Adam lost the image of God temporarily, but Jesus won it back for you! Now Jesus is saying, *"Behold, I give unto YOU power to tread on serpents and scorpions, over all the power of the enemy, and nothing by any means shall harm you"* (Luke 10:19).

It is important that you stand up and tread on the devil who has tried to steal your true image. He will never walk on you again! Begin speaking who you are in Christ. Say, "I always triumph in Christ." Who is Christ in you? He is your hope of glory!

When my daughter Sarah was in the fifth grade, she had a very poor image of herself in the area of sports ability. Every year when her school's "Track and Field Day" arrived, Sarah never won any contests. I used to reassure her, "Well, you can't be good in everything." But one day the Lord told me, "Stop teaching your child unbelief. She can do all things through Christ Who strengthens her."

I repented to God, and to Sarah, and we began saying what the Word says. Sarah had never won any first-place ribbons, but that year she won two of them! Later she joined a basketball team and kept on confessing God's Word. Sarah kept improving, and finally four years later she won an all-star award! What seemed like total failure turned into victory--all because Sarah spoke God's Word, and it came to pass in her life.

See yourself as God sees you. The devil lied to you. But if you remember that God created you as a winner, you can pull unbelief from your heart and sow truth instead. I know that you will triumph in Christ!

MAKE-UP FOR CHRISTIANS

Dear Marilyn:

Do you think it is okay for a Christian woman to wear makeup and, in particular, mascara? Our pastor thinks that women who wear makeup are loose and are just like Jezebel. I am not sure what the Bible teaches on this. I do think that women, especially as they get older, look better if they use at least a little makeup. But I don't want to go against my pastor, and I do want to be a Christian woman who brings glory to the name of Jesus.

Dear Friend:

Pretty eyes are a becoming feature. But some of us women didn't get that natural beauty that others possess! If a little makeup and darkening of the lashes will cover up some of our bad points and highlight our good ones, I don't think there is anything wrong with it. Likewise, I don't believe there is anything wrong with wearing an attractive outfit or having one's hair styled.

Jezebel painted her face (2 Kings 9:30), but it wasn't her face that was her problem—it was her wicked life. She was a priestess of Baal. She married King Ahab and tried to influence him to give Baal equal rights with the God of Israel. Jezebel was cruel and unscrupulous. She continually manipulated her husband into making ungodly decisions. In addition to practicing witchcraft, Jezebel killed the prophets of Jehovah.

The painting of her eyes was a small thing compared to the terrible acts of her life. With her eyes painted and hair fixed, she finally tried to seduce a man who was attempting to kill her. All her eye paint and all her makeup didn't work. Instead, her intended lover called for some men to throw her out the window! Dogs literally ate her, just as the prophet Elijah had prophesied.

Local customs have a great deal to do with makeup. In some churches I have heard people say it is a sin to wear red! Yet in Proberbs 31:22, we read that a virtuous woman had "her clothing in silk and purple." This indicates to me that she liked bright colors! Silk was expensive, so she must have liked nice things.

Job was eventually blessed by three very beautiful daughters. One of the daughters was named Keren-happuch, which means "horn of eye paint." Evidently she had beautiful eyes, and maybe she even used some color to keep them beautiful!

Probably the number-one thing God wants us to be as Christian women is moderate in the way we use our makeup. I have found that God loves women whether they wear eye makeup or not. In Revelations 3:18b it states that we are to *"anoint thine eyes with eyesalve, that thou mayest see."* It is the spiritual eyes that we need to have opened. They are the most important. May our outward eyes reveal the beauty of Jesus.

Index

abortion, 89-92
adultery, 24, 45-7
anger, 20, 53-4, 117-8

backsliding, 130-1
bad habits, 54-5
bad influences, 44, 56-7
baptism
  of babies 112
  water, 112-3
Bible
  confessing/
    meditating the Word, 102-3
  consistency of reading, 9, 65-8
  which translation, 65-6
bitterness, 10-11, 37-9, 69-71, 110-2, 117-8, 132-3
blessing others, 101-2
body, problems with, 14, 22, 54-5, 57-8, 145-6

carnal desire, 24, 45-8, 54-6, 120-1, 127-8 (see also *lusts, materialistic behavior*)
carnal nature (see *"sense" nature*)
charismatic movement, 107
charity, 109-110, 139
child abuse, 19
children
  church attendance of 26-7
  discipline, 19-20
  "joy" of parents, 11-13
  of adult age, 11-12
  "quality time" with, 15-16
  rebellious, 24-7
  religious teaching, 19-27
  self-confidence, 22-3, 144
  sexual problems, 24-5, 44-5, 48-50
  unborn, 89-90
  unsaved, 24-5
Christians
  backsliding, inconsistent, 66-9, 128-131
  materialistic (see *materialistic behavior*)
  political involvement of, 91-2
  unchristian, 127-8, 131-4
  unsupportive, 117-8

church
  attendance, 9, 26-7, 109
  charity of, 109-110, 139
  criticism of, 27, 117-9
  nonsupportive, 117-8
  positive attitude toward, 26-7, 113-4
  women in, 14-16, 107-8
cigarette smoking, 54-5
cleansing of sin, 86-8, 93
clothing, 10, 134-5
condemnation of self (see *self-image*)
congregation
  critical of minister, 110-2
  nonsupportive of fellow members, 117-8
controlling your life, 89-92
correspondence, dealing with, 142-3
criticism of others, 92-3, 102-4, 110-2, 119-120

dancing in church, 81
dating, 13-14
death, 37-8, 78-9
  sin unto, 85-6
  suicide, 88-9
  abortion, 89-92
defeatism (see *self-image*)
demons, casting out, 98-9
"dirty" thoughts and jokes, 47-8, 56
discipline, 19-20
disillusionment with God, 78-9
divorces, 113-4
doctrines, false, 34-6
dreams, 47-8
drugs, 24

enemies, 101-2, 110-2

faith, 79, 89, 103-4, 122-3
failure, 22-3, 59-60, 143-5 (see *self-image*)
false doctrine (see *doctrine, false*)
fears, 14
financial problems, 10-11, 93
food, 57-9
foolishness, 20

149

Index

fornication, 24, 43-7, 85
freedom from carnal habits, 54-56 (see *carnal desires, "sense" nature*)
fruits of the Spirit, 53

giving (see *charity*)
goals, 141
God's will/voice, 76-8, 97-8
gossip, 56, 92-3, 110-1, 119-120, 133
grief, 37-9

healing, 78-80, 101-1
husband (Christian), 9-16, 21, 53-4, 86-7
hypocrites, 132-3

idleness, 58 (see also, *lazy*)
impossible situations, 128-130
inadequacies (see *self-image*)
incest, 85
inconsistency of Christian behavior, 20, 66-7, 128-130
in-laws, 36-7

judging others (see *criticism of others*)

lazy, 23, 123-4
lesbian, 48-50
losers (see *self-image*)
lusts, carnal, 24, 43-50, 56-8, 77
lying, 86
makeup, 145-6
marriage, 9-14, 32, 43-7
materialistic behavior, 10-11, 102-4, 131-2, 134-5
mature Christians, 56
meditating the Word, 103-4
mental attitudes, 56-7
ministers
  evil gossip about, 119-120
  unscriptural behavior of, 118-9
  unsupportive behavior by, 117-8
  women as, 14-15
  "ministry" or calling, 15, 109-110
  desiring ministries of others, 120-2
  of yourself, 98-100, 113-4, 121-4

ministries
  gossip about, 119-120
  staff problems, 122-24
miracles, 12, 26
money (see *financial problems*)
mother, 113-4 (see *wife*)
mouth, controlling yours, 54
murder, 88-92
murmuring, 123 (see *negative words, gossip, criticism of others*)

negative words against Christians, 9, 119-120 (see *ridicule of belief*)
neighbors, 21
"new man," 70

offenses by others, 60-1, 86-8, 101-2, 110-2
office problems, 45-7, 108
opportunities, how to take advantage of, 113-4, 128-9, 140-1
organization of time, 140

parenting (see *wife, husband, mother*)
pastor (see *minister*)
patience, 97, 100-1
personality, formation of, 89-92 (see *self-image*)
placing others before God, 11
"playing God," 90-1
political involvement by Christians, 91-2
positive reinforcement, 23, 27, 59-60
potential (achieving yours), 24
praise, loud, 80-1
prayer, 71-2, 75-81
  consistency of, 75-6
  healing, 78-80, 100-1
  God's voice/will, 76-8, 97-8
  length, 75-6
  long distance, 79-80
  loud *vs.* silent, 71-2, 80-1
  time of day, 75
premarital sex, 43-4
procrastination, 141
promiscuity, 24, 43-7, 85

150

Index

prophecy, false, 35, 134-5
"put-downs," 60-1 (see *ridicule of belief*)

rapture, 68-9
rebellion, 21, 24, 26, 32
regret, 86-88
reinforcement of others, 92-3
relationships (see *relatives, wife, husband, children, minister, congregation, dating, in-laws, Christians, enemies*)
relatives, salvation of, 9-10, 24, 31-2, 37-9, 130-1
repentance, 85-88, 92
resentment, 10 (see *bitterness*)
responsibility, familial, 109
retaliation, 11
revelation knowledge, 67-8
ridicule of beliefs, 21, 33-4, 60-1

salvation of relatives (see *relatives salvation of*)
Satan, overcoming, 93 (see *lusts, bad influences, self-image, sex,* and other behavior problems)
scheduling, 124, 139-141
scripture (see *Bible*), 48
self-image (confidence vs. condemnation), 22-3, 59-61, 124, 143-5
"sense" nature/knowledge, 38, 70-1, 76-8, 127-130
service, 76, 108
sex, 43-50
siblings, 60-1
signs, 77-8
sin, 85-93
  unrepented, 85
  unto death, 85-6
singles, 13, 113-4
sinners, confrontation of, 45, 92-3
smoking, 54-5
soul, spirit, 69-71
spanking, 19-20
"standing in the gap," 93
stepchildren, 21
stewardship, 110 (see *service, charity*)

strength, spiritual, 21-2
suicide, 88-9
supportive of others, 92-3

teacher-student problems, 48-50
temper (see *anger*)
temptation, 45-7, 118 (see *lusts, carnal desires*)
thoughts, carnal/unclean, 47-8
time budgeting, 139-143
tithing, 110
tribulation, 68-9
trusting God, 37

unbelievers, 13, 21 (see also *relatives, salvation of*)

vanity, 144-6
virginity, 43-4

weaknesses, 54-8
weight problem, 57-9
wife (Christian), 9-16, 21, 53-4, 86-7
wisdom, 132
women in ministry, 14-16, 107-8
Word, the (see *Bible*)
"works," 87-8 (see *service, charity*)
worship, 80-1

Notes

Notes

Notes

Notes

Receive Jesus Christ as Lord and Savior of Your Life.

The Bible says, *"That if thou shalt confess with thy mouth the Lord Jesus, and shalt believe in thine heart that God hath raised him from the dead, thou shalt be saved. For with the heart man believeth unto righteousness; and with the mouth confession is made unto salvation"* (Romans 10:9,10).

To receive Jesus Christ as Lord and Savior of your life, sincerely pray this prayer from your heart:

Dear Jesus,

I believe that You died for me and that You rose again on the third day. I confess to You that I am a sinner and that I need Your love and forgiveness. Come into my life, forgive my sins, and give me eternal life. I confess You now as my Lord. Thank You for my salvation!

Signed _____

Date _____

Write to us.
We will send you information to help you with your new life in Christ.

Marilyn Hickey Ministries • P.O. Box 17340
Denver, CO 80217 • (303) 770-0400

For Your Information

Free Monthly Magazine

☐ Please send me your free monthly magazine OUTPOURING (including daily devotionals, timely articles, and ministry updates!)

Tapes and Books

☐ Please send me Marilyn's latest product catalog.

Name Miss/Mrs./Mr._____
Please Print

Address_____

City_____

State_____ Zip_____

Phone (_____)_____

Mail to
Marilyn Hickey Ministries
P.O. Box 17340
Denver, CO 80217

Prayer Requests

Let us join our faith with yours for your prayer needs. Fill out below and send to

Marilyn Hickey Ministries
P.O. Box 17340
Denver, CO 80217

Prayer Request_____

_____

_____

_____

_____

_____

Name (Mr. & Mrs. / Mr. / Miss / Mrs.) _____

Address_____

City_____

State_____ Zip_____

Phone (H) ( ) _____

(W) ( ) _____

☐ If you want prayer immediately, call our Prayer Center at (303) 796-1333, Monday – Friday, 4:00 am – 8:00 pm (MT).

TOUCHING YOU WITH THE LOVE OF JESUS!

Marilyn Hickey PRAYER CENTER

When was the last time that you could say, "He touched me, right where I hurt"? No matter how serious the nature of your call, we're here to pray the Word and show you how to touch Jesus for real answers to real problems.

Call us, and let's touch Jesus, together!

(303) 796-1333

Open Mon. – Fri., 4:00 am – 8:00 pm (MT).

WE CARE!

BOOKS BY MARILYN HICKEY

A CRY FOR MIRACLES ($5.95)
ACTS ($7.95)
ANGELS ALL AROUND ($7.95)
BEAT TENSION ($.75)
BIBLE CAN CHANGE YOU, THE ($12.95)
BOLD MEN WIN ($.75)
BREAK THE GENERATION CURSE ($7.95)
BULLDOG FAITH ($.75)
CHANGE YOUR LIFE ($.75)
CHILDREN WHO HIT THE MARK ($.75)
CONQUERING SETBACKS ($.75)
DAILY DEVOTIONAL ($5.95)
DEAR MARILYN ($5.95)
DIVORCE IS NOT THE ANSWER ($4.95)
ESPECIALLY FOR TODAY'S WOMAN ($14.95)
EXPERIENCE LONG LIFE ($.75)
FASTING & PRAYER ($.75)
FREEDOM FROM BONDAGES ($4.95)
GIFT-WRAPPED FRUIT ($2.00)
GOD'S BENEFIT: HEALING ($.75)
GOD'S COVENANT FOR YOUR FAMILY ($5.95)
GOD'S RX FOR A HURTING HEART ($3.50)
GOD'S SEVEN KEYS TO MAKE YOU RICH ($.75)
HOLD ON TO YOUR DREAM ($.75)
HOW TO BECOME A MATURE CHRISTIAN ($5.95)
HOW TO BECOME MORE THAN A CONQUEROR ($.75)
HOW TO WIN FRIENDS ($.75)
I CAN BE BORN AGAIN AND SPIRIT FILLED ($.75)
I CAN DARE TO BE AN ACHIEVER ($.75)
KEYS TO HEALING REJECTION ($.75)
KNOW YOUR MINISTRY ($3.50)
MAXIMIZE YOUR DAY . . . GOD'S WAY ($7.95)
NAMES OF GOD ($7.95)
#1 KEY TO SUCCESS—MEDITATION ($3.50)
POWER OF FORGIVENESS, THE ($.75)
POWER OF THE BLOOD, THE ($.75)
RECEIVING RESURRECTION POWER ($.75)
RENEW YOUR MIND ($.75)
SATAN-PROOF YOUR HOME ($7.95)
"SAVE THE FAMILY" PROMISE BOOK ($14.95)
SIGNS IN THE HEAVENS ($4.95)
SOLVING LIFE'S PROBLEMS ($.75)
SPEAK THE WORD ($.75)
STANDING IN THE GAP ($.75)
STORY OF ESTHER, THE ($.75)
WINNING OVER WEIGHT ($.75)
WOMEN OF THE WORD ($.75)
YOUR MIRACLE SOURCE ($3.50)
YOUR PERSONALITY WORKOUT ($5.95)

MARILYN HICKEY BIBLE COLLEGE

Explore your options and increase your knowledge of the Word at this unique college of higher learning for men and women of faith. The Marilyn Hickey Bible College offers **on-campus and correspondence courses** that give you the opportunity to learn from Marilyn Hickey and other great Bible scholars, who can help prepare you to be an effective minister of the gospel. Classes are available for both full- and part-time students.

For more information, complete the coupon below and send to

**Marilyn Hickey Bible College
P.O. Box 17340
Denver, CO 80217
(303) 770-0400**

Please print.

Name (Mr./Mrs./Miss) _____

Address_____

City _____ State_____ Zip_____

Phone (H) ( ) _____ (W) ( ) _____